A Purbeck Romance

A Purbeck Romance

Set in Thomas Hardy's Glorious Wessex

ANDREW NORMAN

ryelands

First published in Great Britain in 2023

Copyright © Andrew Norman
Cover design: George Kalchev

British Library Cataloguing-in-Publication Data
A CIP record for this title is available from the British Library

ISBN 978 1 906551 52 0

Ryelands
Halsgrove House,
Ryelands Business Park,
Bagley Road, Wellington, Somerset TA21 9PZ
Tel: 01823 653777 Fax: 01823 216796
email: sales@halsgrove.com

FSC
www.fsc.org
MIX
Paper | Supporting
responsible forestry
FSC® C122244

Part of the Halsgrove group of companies
Information on all Halsgrove titles is available at:
www.halsgrove.com

Printed and bound in India by Parksons Graphics Ltd

Contents

To my dearly beloved wife
Alison Rachel Norman:

The Love of My Life
The Light of My Life
My Precious Lamb

About the Author

Andrew Norman was born in Newbury, Berkshire, UK in 1943. Having been educated at Thornhill High School, Gwelo, Southern Rhodesia (now Zimbabwe), Midsomer Norton Grammar School, and St Edmund Hall, Oxford, he qualified in medicine at the Radcliffe Infirmary. He has two children Bridget and Thomas, by his first wife.

From 1972-83, Andrew worked as a general practitioner in Poole, Dorset, before a spinal injury cut short his medical career. He is now an established writer whose published works include biographies of Charles Darwin, Winston Churchill, Thomas Hardy, T. E. Lawrence, Adolf Hitler, Agatha Christie, Enid Blyton, Beatrix Potter, and Sir Arthur Conan Doyle. Andrew married his second wife Rachel in 2005.

By the same author

By Swords Divided: Corfe Castle in the Civil War. Halsgrove, 2003.
Thomas Hardy: Christmas Carollings. Halsgrove, 2005.
Enid Blyton and her Enchantment with Dorset. Halsgrove, 2005.
Tyneham: A Tribute. Halsgrove, 2007.
Agatha Christie: The Finished Portrait. Tempus, 2007.
The Story of George Loveless and the Tolpuddle Martyrs. Halsgrove, 2008.
Father of the Blind: A Portrait of Sir Arthur Pearson. The History Press, 2009.
Agatha Christie: The Pitkin Guide. Pitkin Publishing, 2009.
Arthur Conan Doyle: The Man behind Sherlock Holmes. The History Press,
    2009.
HMS Hood: Pride of the Royal Navy. The History Press, 2009.
Purbeck Personalities. Halsgrove, 2009.
Bournemouth's Founders and Famous Visitors. The History Press, 2010.
Thomas Hardy: Behind the Mask. The History Press, 2011.
A Brummie Boy goes to War. Halsgrove, 2011.
Hitler: Dictator or Puppet? Pen & Sword, 2011.
Winston Churchill: Portrait of an Unquiet Mind. Pen & Sword Books, 2012.
Charles Darwin: Destroyer of Myths. Pen & Sword Books, 2013.
Beatrix Potter: Her Inner World. Pen & Sword Books, 2013.
T.E. Lawrence: Tormented Hero. Fonthill, 2014.
Agatha Christie: The Disappearing Novelist. Fonthill, 2014.
Lawrence of Arabia's Clouds Hill. Halsgrove, 2014.
Jane Austen: Love is Like a Rose. Fonthill, 2015.
Kindly Light: The Story of Blind Veterans UK. Fonthill, 2015.
Thomas Hardy at Max Gate: The Latter Years. Halsgrove, 2016.
Corfe Remembered. Halsgrove, 2017.
Thomas Hardy: Bockhampton and Beyond. Halsgrove, 2017.
Mugabe: Monarch of Blood and Tears. Austin Macauley, 2017
Making Sense of Marilyn. Fonthill, 2018.
Hitler's Insanity: A Conspiracy of Silence. Fonthill, 2018.
The Unwitting Fundamentalist. Austin Macauley, 2018.
Robert Mugabe's Lost Jewel of Africa. Fonthill, 2018.
Halsewell: A Shipwreck that Gripped the Nation. Fonthill, 2020.
Beatrix Potter: Her Inner World. Pen & Sword Books, 2020.
*The Amazing Story of Lise Meitner: Escaping the Nazis and becoming the
    World's Greatest Physicist.* Pen & Sword Books, 2021.

Author's website https://www.andrew-norman.co.uk

Author's Note

'Corfe Castle' is the name for both the village of Corfe and for its castle. As regards the village, 'Corfe' and 'Corfe Castle' are regarded as interchangeable in the following narrative.

1

A Blind Date

IT WAS getting light. I got up, went to the window, and drew back the curtains. I could see Poole Harbour and the sunshine on the water and on the distant hills beyond, giving the promise of a lovely day to come. Could this be the day, *the* day, when it actually happens? But be realistic Andrew, I told myself. You have been at this game for a long while now!

It was not my habit to wear a watch, so I kept an eye on the clock. It was already 9.30 a.m., and I was due to meet up with a lady on a blind date at 11. Better get a move on!

As regards the forthcoming date, I suppose I was fairly 'laid back'. I had hopes, yes, certainly, but little expectation that it would be a success, based on my past experience with the 'fairer sex'. What was the tally so far? 83 successive blind dates over a three-year period, with little or nothing to show for it. True, I had acquired several lady friends over that period, but nothing had lasted; nothing had really gelled.

I dressed hastily, taking no particular care as to what clothes I wore, I must confess. Don't invest in failure, my late father had always taught me! I put on my anorak, just in case of rain, and a pair of trainers, both of which had seen better days. And now, time to set off! I had decided to go by bicycle and left myself about an hour to get there, which should have been ample.

I locked the front door of my bungalow from the inside, exited via the garage (where I kept my bike), tucked my trousers into my socks (where were those elusive cycle clips?), locked the garage door and set off for the ferry, pedalling in leisurely fashion. The harbour soon came into view, spread out before me in all its glory.

A car ferry plied regularly to-and-fro across the harbour entrance, between South Dorsetshire's Sandbanks peninsula and the so-called, Isle of Purbeck – usually referred to simply as 'Purbeck' – which is actually not an island at all. However, on my arrival, there was clearly a delay. I could see the ferry floating motionless on the far side, when by now it should have arrived at my side. I guessed that it was waiting for a ship, one which was about to exit the harbour, there being none visible out at sea. Meanwhile, I purchased my ticket from the ticket machine. Sure enough, after a few minutes, a large vessel duly hove into view, sailing between Sandbanks and Brownsea Island en route for France.

Finally, the ferry arrived, discharged its cargo of cars, and began loading up once more. I went aboard and wheeled my bicycle into the area designated for 'Cycles and Motorcycles'. Finally, I climbed the stairs to enjoy the views: from the upper deck, of the harbour and its islands on the one side, and the sparkling waters of Poole Bay and the open sea on the other. 'Chug, chug, chug' went the motor, as it engaged the chains which would drive the ferry slowly but surely across to the other side.

Having no wish to be mown down by the traffic, I waited until all the vehicles had disembarked, before setting off on the long, straight road which lay before me. It was the 6th of June, the anniversary of D-Day, when sixty years previously, Allied forces had massed in several locations in this vicinity, prior to crossing the English Channel on a mission to liberate Europe from the clutches of Nazi Germany. I did not know it at the time, but 6 June would also be a day that I would thereafter always have cause to remember.

The grass was parched, the only greenery in sight being in the distance, where trees abutted onto a lake which, at some time in history, had formed when it was cut off from sea. The delay at the ferry had set me back, so I began pedalling faster, along an uphill gradient to the bend in the road where deer were apt to cross at dusk; then on, down the hill and up again to the little village of Studland. And now I had almost reached my destination: the place of the arranged rendezvous being a hotel, which lay just ahead on the near side of the road.

I cycled brusquely into the car park and dismounted, but to my surprise, there was not a single motor vehicle in sight. Had I been 'stood up', I wondered? Or had the lady in question come on foot? Up until now, we had only spoken briefly on the phone, and I had no idea where she lived, though I guessed it must be hereabouts as the rendezvous was her suggestion.

It was then that I spotted a small white Fiat, almost hidden under the drooping branches of a willow tree. Could this be her, I wondered? I walked towards it, and on my approach the occupant, a female, wound down the window. 'Is it Rachel?' I asked. 'You must be Andrew,' she replied, emerging from the vehicle. Whereupon, I observed that she was reasonably tall, but not quite as tall as myself. That was a relief! A previous lady whom I had met on a blind date, had towered over me by at least 4 inches! 'Am I late?' I enquired. She looked at her watch and frowned. Not a good beginning, I said to myself, and I apologized. 'I'm so sorry.' I stood my bike by the front porch, locked it, and pushed the heavy oak front door open for her.

'Did you have far to come?' I asked.

'I live in Herston,' she replied. This was a hamlet situated a mile or so to the west of the coastal town of Swanage. 'And you?'

'I live in Poole,' I said.

'So you came over on the ferry?' I nodded.

She chose a seat for us in the lounge by the window, where double doors opened onto a spacious lawn, with the sea beyond. I was pleased that the hotel, which I had visited many times before, had not been 'modernized', and that the room was as cosy and homely as ever with its original fireplace, old-fashioned furniture, and equally old-fashioned paintings of pastoral scenes hanging on the wall. I much preferred to live in the past, rather than in the present. Somehow, I felt safer there,

We sat opposite to one another, and I took the opportunity to study Rachel more closely. She was dressed modestly, but elegantly, in grey skirt and pale-pink blouse, and around her neck hung a cameo brooch. She wore little make up. She had no need to, for I saw at once that she was a natural beauty, with fair, wavy hair and hazel eyes. To see her so smartly attired made me feel ashamed, well, almost, that I had not made more of an effort myself!

During the course of the conversation, I learned that she, like me, was a divorcee.

'How long have you lived in these parts, Rachel?' I enquired.

'Several years,' she replied.

'And you, Andrew?'

'The same.'

'Have you any family?'

'A daughter,' she replied. 'But she lives in Canada.'

'I have a son,' I said, 'but he is on the other side of the world, in Australia.'

The waiter approached and we ordered a cafetière for two, which soon appeared, served in the traditional manner with genuine china cups, milk jug, and sugar bowl complete with tongs.

'Shall I be mother?' Rachel asked when the coffee had brewed.

Having ascertained that I preferred it white, she commenced pouring the milk. However, as she did so, a few drops, amounting probably to less than a teaspoonful, spilled onto the table. A look of anguish came over her face and, to my surprise, she summoned the waiter who looked bemused when she pointed to the spilt milk. He returned with a cloth and mopped it up with perhaps a slightly exaggerated flourish!

Rachel told me that she had once been a nursing sister. That explains her meticulousness, I thought. This was a strange coincidence I said, because I had once been a general medical practitioner – or

'G.P.'. What I did not reveal to her was that I had been obliged to give up work some years previously and well before my time, after sustaining what is commonly known as a 'slipped disc'. It was only after several botched operations that the final one was successful. However, I was left with a degree of residual sciatica which caused me pain after prolonged sitting. But when walking a modest distance, or bicycling, I was relatively pain free. For the moment, however, I did not let on about my ailment. To do so, I thought, might be to risk the dreaded big 'R' – 'Rejection!'. As for Rachel, she told me that she had been a senior nursing sister in a top London hospital, but she now worked from home, proofreading medical journals.

After coffee, I took the opportunity to visit the gents, and swallow a couple of painkillers. The bill arrived, and I was impressed when she offered to pay. However, I thanked her for her kind offer, but declined it.

As we exited through the double doors and onto the lawn, I sensed that the moment of truth was rapidly approaching. Will she make some excuse and quickly depart, I wondered, having little self-confidence?

2

A Walk Along the Beach

AFTER A pregnant silence, I found myself saying, somewhat nervously, 'I wonder if you would care to take a little walk by the sea with me?'

'Yes, I should like that. Thank you,' Rachel replied quietly.

Was it my imagination, or did she blush?

We set off down the path and duly arrived at the beach, where the waves made gentle, soothing sounds as they lapped the shore; the only other living creatures in sight, apart from ourselves, being a gaggle of seagulls, pecking away in the sand and squawking at each other beside the water's edge.

We made our way along the beach and came to a boat-launching ramp, which, as it was high tide, occupied its whole width. I approached the ramp first and as I did so, she took my arm to steady me as I clambered up and over it. This thoughtful gesture on her part made a lasting impression. Whereupon, I did the same for her.

At the far end of the beach was a kiosk, where I bought us both an ice cream. This we enjoyed sitting on a wooden bench and taking in the tranquility of the scene. That was before the seagulls descended on us in a cacophony of sound. I wondered what was going on in her mind? It all seemed too good to be true! On some previous blind dates I had encountered indifference, and sometimes even outright hostility. Yet this quiet, thoughtful, and obviously intelligent woman seemed relaxed and friendly.

As we retraced our steps, however, I found myself becoming increasingly apprehensive. It was always a problem, when these kind of dates came to an end, to know what to say. Be too inhibited, and the opportunity may pass; be too forward, and one risked getting hurt.

Rachel stood by her car, but instead of getting in and speeding away into the wide, blue yonder as I feared she might, she stood silently waiting.

'I have enjoyed meeting you,' I said. 'Perhaps you would like to meet again sometime?'

Each second seemed an eternity until, breaking the silence, she said, to my relief and surprise, 'Yes, I would. Thank you.'

How am I to contact her, I wondered? For, whereas I had included *my* telephone number in the advertisement which I had placed in the personal column of the newspaper, to which she had responded, I did not have hers.

The advertisement, which had brought the two of us together, had been composed by my friend Graham. It was brief and to the point. 'Distinguished Dorset Doctor seeks female companion. Enjoys visiting the countryside and stately homes.' 'The mention of stately homes always attracts the right sort of person,' Graham had told me. As for the word 'distinguished', was this not rather pretentious, I asked him? 'Not at all. You have to sell yourself!' he insisted. Meanwhile, before I had plucked up the courage to ask Rachel for it, she had written her phone number down on a piece of paper for me.

Having arrived back at my bungalow I reflected on the meeting, and that one incident that had stood out for me: the gesture of Rachel's when she had helped me to negotiate the boat ramp. Surely, this was indicative of a caring nature, I thought.

It seemed absurd, because we had been together for a period of less than three hours, and yet images of Rachel filled my mind. It was as if I had been taken over! That steadfast gaze as it met my eyes; how she had spontaneously taken my hand as we retraced our steps along the beach; her graceful, feminine demeanor and movements. Why, even when she stood still, with her weight mainly on one leg, and the other knee bent and resting against the other, this was all part of her feminine allure. If I do not hear from her, I decided, I will telephone her in about a week or two's time. It won't do to give her the impression that I am too eager, now will it?

I found that food did not interest me. I switched on the television but was unable to concentrate. Finally, I yielded to temptation and picked up the phone, only to be met with a disembodied voice. It was Rachel's answerphone. Is she there, but deliberately not answering, I wondered? Is this her way of giving me the old heave-ho?

I took a deep breath and addressed the machine. 'Rachel, it's me, Andrew. Just to say I hope you got back safely. Do let me know when we can meet again, if you so wish.' I then poured myself a large glass of red wine. I hoped that I had not sounded too desperate or impatient, but patience never was my strong point!

That same evening, I was snoozing on the settee when the telephone rang. It was Rachel. She had not returned my call sooner, she said, because she had been to the dentist. Having exchanged pleasantries, we agreed to meet in three days' time. I would come over once again to Purbeck on the ferry and, weather permitting, we would visit a local beauty spot on the coast. Three whole days! How would I survive, I wondered?

Since my back injury I had taken up writing, and as I worked away on my latest book, time passed slowly. On the one hand, I looked forward with pleasurable anticipation to meeting Rachel again, but on the other, there was a nagging doubt in the back of my mind. Would she cry off at the last minute? Had it all been only a dream?

3

An Assignation in Purbeck

IN RESPECT of my forthcoming meeting with Rachel I was determined, on this occasion, to be punctual and to dress smartly, despite the fact that sartorial elegance was not my strong point! Once again, it was a beautiful, cloudless day. A coat would therefore not be necessary. However, I decided to take my haversack, in which I placed my groundsheet. This might come in useful if my back played up.

This time, the journey across the ferry was uneventful, and I motored along in my Land Rover through the rolling Dorset countryside until I reached the rendezvous: a car park set on a hilltop above the village of Worth Matravers – or 'Worth'. I espied Rachel, sitting in her white Fiat saloon. It was 11:55 a.m. by the Land Rover's clock, but once again, she had arrived before me. I parked alongside and waved. Whereupon, she emerged from her car and approached with a smile.

Throughout the journey I had been listening to an episode of Thomas Hardy's novel, *Far From the Madding Crowd* on BBC Radio 4. Farmer Gabriel Oak has proposed marriage to Bathsheba Everdene, saying, 'at home by the fire, whenever you look up, there I shall be – and whenever I look up there will be you.' To this, she replies, 'Wait, wait, and don't be improper!' Could this be some kind of prophesy, I asked myself? I got out of the car and once again beheld Rachel's lovely face. Will she be my 'Bathsheba' one day, I wondered? But then came the voice of reason. 'Don't be silly, Andrew. You hardly know her!'

We set off together on foot, down the narrow lane towards Worth, and paused for a while to watch the ducks on the duck pond. Before us was a long, winding track to be negotiated, with many loose stones. She led the way, pausing every so often in her usual thoughtful manner when we encountered an extra steep section, and taking my arm. Finally, before us, was Winspit.

This was the site of a former cliff quarry, from where stone was transported, but not by horse and wagon. Instead, it was lowered down the cliff face by means of a derrick (or 'whim') into boats ('lighters') waiting below, an extremely hazardous procedure.

As I gazed in rapture at the sparkling sea below, I took the liberty of putting my arm around Rachel's waist. She did not demur, and I marvelled at the softness of her flesh, which was easily palpable through the thin, cotton dress that she was wearing.

We came to a wide, rocky ledge, created by centuries of quarrying. Here were great, man-made caves, with an occasional pillar, left in situ to prevent collapse of the roof. By now, my back was beginning to ache, but I did not let on. However, with the trained eye of a former nursing sister, she noticed by the strained look on my face that something was wrong.

'Let's rest here a while,' she said.

I spread the groundsheet out on the flat, rocky surface, and lay down. Rachel looked at me somewhat quizzically, hesitating before sitting down at my side. It was no good. She was not to be fooled.

'You are in pain, aren't you,' she said insightfully. 'Is it your back?' I nodded.

She rummaged around in her handbag, brought out a packet of wafer biscuits, and offered me one. Whereupon, a pigeon flew down and had the temerity to approach to within an arm's length of the groundsheet.

'Shoo it away,' I said.

'No, I shan't, poor thing!' she said, breaking off a small piece of her biscuit and throwing it towards 'Mr Pigeon' – or was it a 'Mrs'?

This procedure was repeated several times over. The greedy bird will hardly be able to take off after all that lot, I thought. And then I remembered what my dear late mother had once told me: that people who were kind to animals were generally kind to other people.

From my recumbent position, I took the opportunity to study her, whilst she remained preoccupied with the pigeon. What perfume is that she's wearing, I wondered, and guessed that it was an expensive one.

'Would you like to go on further?' I enquired, my pain having somewhat diminished.

We followed the path eastwards, towards the top of the cliff. It was narrow, and there was a sheer drop. The waves churned below, and although they were fairly benign, I knew that anyone who missed their footing here, would have little chance of survival.

'Keep well in,' I advised.

Shortly afterwards we arrived at Seacombe, another former cliff quarry; this time with a rocky ledge that was situated just above sea level and sloped downwards to where the waves were gently breaking. As I spread out the groundsheet once again, I observed that we were alone, but not for long. For suddenly, to our surprise, there was that pigeon again: recognizable by its markings as being the very same one that we had encountered previously. It must have managed to take off, after all, I concluded! Whereupon, Rachel's performance with the wafer biscuits was repeated!

This time, Rachel lay down beside me. It was not only her features that I admired, but also her figure; slender at the waist, yet well rounded in all the right places. She subsequently let slip that in her younger days, she had done some modelling, and had once appeared in *Harper's Bazaar* magazine.

We made our way back up a long, winding path, through the lush Dorsetshire countryside, so beloved of Thomas Hardy. Little did we know at the time, but the famous Dorset poet and novelist of yesteryear was shortly to play a significant part in both our lives.

We held hands almost all of the way, but occasionally, where the path was narrow, she walked in front. Her posture, and the graceful manner in which she moved, were doubtless a legacy of her modelling days. Could it be that I have fallen in love I wondered? Was this possible, after so short an acquaintance? But try not to get carried away, I said to myself. After all, things might still go wrong, and you might yet face rejection, though as yet there was no indication of it, judging by the loving looks that she gave me. But past experience had taught me that in every 'Garden of Eden', there frequently lurked a serpent!

After a visit to the tearooms, we returned to the car park. What was in her mind, I wondered, not wishing to make the first move? Suddenly, to my surprise and delight, she reached up and kissed me.

'I have so much enjoyed the day,' she said.

'Me, likewise. Thank you.'

I gave her a long hug.

Hesitating for a moment, she said, 'Forgive me if I am being too forward, but I am due to visit Poole next week, as I have some shopping to do there. Will you be about, and if so, may I please call in?'

Overcome by a mixture of excitement and emotion, and not trusting myself to find the right words, I merely nodded at her and smiled. It was as if, after a long period in the desert, I had finally encountered an oasis!

When Rachel visited my bungalow a few days later I made us a pot of tea and offered her some lardy cake which I had purchased at the local supermarket. Cooking, let alone cake-making, was definitely not my forte! Since the divorce, my main meal of the day had been a cooked English breakfast, consumed at the local 'Greasy Spoon' café. She politely declined the lardy cake and I deduced that she was particular about what she ate: hence her trim figure.

Once or twice, in the lounge, I noticed Rachel looking about herself with a somewhat bemused expression, and all the more so when I showed her into the kitchen.

'So you don't employ a cleaner then?' she said.

The answer was, 'No, afraid not.'

'I hope you don't mind me asking', she said, 'but do you happen to possess a vacuum cleaner?' Did I detect a note of sarcasm in her voice?

'Er... I think it might be in the hall cupboard,' I replied bashfully. Oh dear, I thought, another black mark! The truth was, that all I had done since moving into the bungalow several years previously was to slap a coat of paint on the walls.

That evening, Rachel telephoned me from her home in Herston.

'Thank you for having me,' she said. I took the proverbial bull by the horns.

'Would you care to come over again one day,' I asked. 'If you chose a sunny day, we could sit by the pond and have tea.'

'That would be lovely,' she said.

4

Rachel Returns: The Works of Thomas Hardy

WHEN RACHEL next visited me at my bungalow in Poole, she quickly made her presence felt! In the bathroom, laundry room, and kitchen, a vast array of household cleaning materials appeared as if by magic. She even purchased some beeswax, presumably in order to spruce up my antique secretaire bookcase.

'Will you be seeing your friend Graham today?' she said, dropping a broad hint.

And I realized that she was desperate to get me out of the house for a while, in order that she could get to work on the bungalow and begin the mammoth task of removing years of accumulated grime. And almost before I had exited through the front door, I heard the sound of the vacuum cleaner, as it sprang into life.

I have to confess that it afforded me great pleasure, when certain 'ladies' items' began to appear. In the bathroom, for example, bubble bath, and several varieties of shampoo; and on the bedroom dressing table, lipstick, moisturizing cream, hairspray, conditioner, nail varnish, etc., etc.

Before I knew it, I was frogmarched by Rachel to the shops to purchase a new pair of trainers, new shirts and trousers, and not one, but three anoraks, one for summer, one for winter, and one for best, she said.

When I did offer to help, all I was entrusted with were modest tidying up jobs in the garden, as long as I did not succumb to my normal impulse of wanting to chop everything down; and such menial tasks as loading or unloading the dishwasher or bringing the weekly shopping in from the car. But how I appreciated her, as she attended to her various self-appointed tasks. My home had truly come alive.

'Do you possess *any* books that are not either written by Thomas Hardy or written about him?' asked Rachel with a smile, as she examined my bookcase?

'There are dozens more in the loft,' I said.

'Hardy preferred to be thought of primarily as a poet, rather than a novelist, am I right?' she said.

After lunch, we sat together drinking wine.

'So why the obsession with Hardy?' she asked.

'Perhaps it's because my paternal ancestors came from Fordington, Dorchester,' I said. 'Which is not far from Higher Bockhampton where Hardy was born, and not far from Max Gate where he lived with his wife, Emma.' Said Rachel, 'so Hardy is in your DNA?' 'Not quite, but almost,' I said.

5

An Invitation to Purbeck

AT THE end of Rachel's stay, it was agreed that I would follow her in convoy back to Herston. 'Shall we have lunch at Durlston Castle?' she asked.

The castle was built in 1887-8 by Swanage stone-magnate, George Burt as a place where he could entertain his visitors, and no doubt show off in the process. Burt's aim was to transform Swanage from a fishing village and port into a fashionable seaside spa. It is situated spectacularly on the edge of the cliffs, just to the south of Swanage on the southern side of Durlston Bay. The castle is now a visitor centre, part of the 280-acre Durlston Country Park and National Nature Reserve, owned by Dorset County Council.

As Rachel and I enjoyed a coffee together, sitting on the terrace overlooking Durlston Bay, our eyes met and I knew from my involuntary reactions, including 'butterflies in the tummy', that romance was in the air!

'Hardy met Burt once,' I told Rachel. 'And tongue in cheek, called him "The King of Swanage"!'

She laughed. 'Now I'm going to test you,' she said. 'What was Hardy's name for Dorchester?'

'That's easy,' I replied. 'Casterbridge.'

In his novels Hardy used what photographer, Hermann Lea, a friend of his for almost thirty years, called 'counterfeit' place names.

'Poole?' Rachel asked.

'Flatmouth was his original name for Poole,' I replied 'and subsequently, Havenpool'.

'Bere Regis?'

'That would be Kingsbere,' I said, and then I noticed that she had brought a Hardy novel with her and was surreptitiously reading off the names from a page entitled, 'Key to Place names'. 'You're cheating!' I said, and she giggled. 'Have I passed the test?'

'With flying colours!' she replied.

A large ship sailed by. 'Ah, there goes the cross-Channel ferry en route from France to Havenpool,' I said.

Rachel laughed. 'You think like Thomas Hardy, and now you're even beginning to sound like him!' she said.

This wonderful day with Rachel seemed likely to end all too quickly, and I found myself not relishing the prospect of returning home to an empty bungalow. But then came a ray of sunshine!

'Would you like to come home with me, and I'll make us some supper?' she enquired.

'Thank you, but I've no wish to inconvenience you,' I replied. This, of course, was an enormous 'white lie'.

We duly arrived at Rachel's house in Herston and having installed me in the lounge with the newspaper, she immediately began busying herself in the kitchen. As I put my head round the kitchen door to ask if I could help, I noticed that lining the shelves above the kitchen units was a vast array of cookery books, including a complete set of Cordon Bleu manuals. A veritable library of the culinary arts, I thought, and (selfishly) perhaps a good omen for the future! Needless to say, my offer of help was politely declined!

Photographs hung on the wall, and one in particular caught my eye. There was Rachel, captain of her school tennis team, together with her teammates, all attired immaculately in white.

Rachel's bookcase contained travel books and books about Scandinavia and the Vikings, which I deduced were particular interests of hers. But best of all, was when I discovered the complete novels of Thomas Hardy, of which she too possessed copies. And she immediately soared even higher in my estimation!

After a tasty supper of pasta and prawns, prepared by her own fair hand, we settled down in the lounge together on the settee and drank red wine. Rachel and I discussed everything under the sun: our late parents; our families; places we had visited. And as the wine took effect, Rachel's face became more and more flushed, and her eyes positively sparkled!

I was aware that the night was drawing in and that the last ferry was due to leave at 11 p.m. If I missed it, this would mean a long drive back to Poole around the harbour. However, glancing surreptitiously at the mantlepiece clock, I deliberately

Durlston Bay by Ernest Hazlehurst, 1915.

waited until *after* 11 p.m. before feigning surprise by saying, 'Oh gosh! Is that the time?'

She gave me a knowing look. 'Yes, Andrew. I'm afraid you've missed the last ferry. Would you care for a glass of champagne', she asked, much to my surprise. 'And another?' We finished the bottle between us. And then, after a pause, she said quietly, 'Would you like to stay the night?' I did not reply, but simply put my arm around her shoulders and gave her a hug. 'Give me a few minutes, and then come on up,' she said, and proceeded up the stairs.

I awoke in the dead of night. The effects of the champagne had largely worn off, and all my insecurities returned. Will she still feel the same when the new day dawns, I wondered?

When I awoke next morning, I found that Rachel was already up and making breakfast. I lay in her bed for a while, reliving the pleasure of the previous night, as the birds sang, and sunshine streamed in through the window. Can this really be true, I asked myself? It had all happened so quickly! But I need not have worried, because when I greeted her, her face was radiant.

'Thank you so much for last night,' she said. 'It was truly *wonderful!*'

6

Christmas

RACHEL KINDLY invited me to her home in Herston for Christmas and New Year. We had now known each other for six months, and every minute that I had spent in her company was a joy.

I arrived to find that furious preparations were in progress: cooking, cleaning, decorating the tree, wrapping presents, and so forth. However, Christmases for me, and doubtless for millions of others, were bitter-sweet occasions, bringing back memories of people and of times gone by that were now irretrievably lost.

The day passed off peacefully, Rachel having prepared a traditional meal of turkey and all the trimmings, followed by Christmas pudding, which we thoroughly enjoyed. On Boxing Day, however, it was a different story as her house positively heaved with her friends and neighbours, so much so that having lived alone for so long, I felt an overwhelming sense of claustrophobia. So, making my excuses, I set off on foot across the fields for Herston Halt, a stop on the historic Swanage to Corfe Steam Heritage Railway line.

I remained at the station for a while, lost in memories of childhood and the age of steam, when mother used to take me down to the level crossing in Winchester (where we lived), in time to see the London train pass by. The driver would always give us a cheery wave! I was also reminded of the Hornby Dublo model electric train set, which my great-grandmother had given me one Christmas.

By the time I returned the guests had departed. Rachel looked anxious. 'I was thinking of sending out a search party for you,' she said. The truth was that my insecurity, which was never far from the surface, has reared its ugly head. But Rachel seemed to sense this and she gave me a long and tender hug. 'Its all right, Andrew,' she said. 'Everything's going to be all right.'

7

Graham

WHEN I returned home to Poole I paid a visit to my friend, Graham who lived nearby. We had attended the same college at Oxford and had first met at the pigeonhole in the porters lodge, where we collected our post from the same slot: our surnames both beginning with the same letter. He and I became lifelong friends, even though he was studying architecture and I was studying physiology, prior to becoming a medical student. We both enjoyed golf, watching 'Pink Panther' movies, and much else. Graham never married. He had lady friends but was always unwilling to make that final commitment.

Graham made the following observation. 'You look different, Andrew,' he said. 'Yes, I should say that there's is definitely something different about you!'

'I'm wearing new clothes,' I replied. 'Could that be it?'

'No, it's more than that. You've got what they call, a spring in your step.' He smiled knowingly, and began humming the music to the song, 'Falling in Love Again'. 'Have I guessed right?' he said. I smiled and nodded. And then I told him about Rachel.

8

A Setback for Rachel:
A Major Decision

ONE DAY, as I was about to leave my home in Poole for Rachel's home in Herston, I happened to check my telephone answerphone and there was a message. It was from her. 'When you arrive, Andrew, please just walk in. I will leave the door unlocked.' Curious, I thought.

When I did arrive at her house and walk in, there was no one in sight. I called up the stairs, and she answered weakly. I went up to find her lying in bed, with tablets and a glass of water beside her on the bedside table. The curtains had not been drawn and it was almost dark. 'What on earth's wrong?' I said anxiously, and she explained.

'Sometimes my fibromyalgia flares up. I've tried to keep it hidden from you, darling.' She had not called me 'darling' before and I appreciated it more than she knew. 'The doctors can't seem to make it out,' she continued, 'and all they can do is give me painkillers. Otherwise, I just have to wait for it to go. Sometimes the after-effects last for two or three days. And then I'm perfectly all right.' Tears welled up in her eyes. 'You're not going to desert me, are you?'

I kissed her and hugged her gently. 'Do you need anything? I'm just going down to the shops.'

'No, the milkman had been,' she said, 'and there is food in the fridge and freezer.'

'I'll see you in a minute,' I said.

The truth was, that I had seen something in one of the local gift shops that I thought Rachel would like. And this was my opportunity.

It was an ornamental seal, fashioned out of the locally mined and highly-prized Purbeck marble. I wrapped it up nicely, and when she awakened from sleep, I gave it to her.

'It's beautiful,' she said stroking its exquisitely smooth surface.

'Lucky old seal,' I said. Whereupon, she started sobbing.

'You're so kind to me Andrew,' she said.

I spent the next few days doing odd jobs around the house and tidying the garden. She does so much for me, I thought. Now it's payback time. And anxious not to cause her any unnecessary stress, I slept in the adjacent bedroom. Within a fortnight, she had fully recovered.

No one should be alone and have to suffer like this, I said to myself, and then I had a brainwave. I made a decision to relocate to Purbeck. I would purchase a house in Corfe Castle, in the very heart of 'Thomas Hardy Country' and one day, if all went well, I would invite Rachel to come and live with me there. But I did not count my proverbial chickens!

And as luck would have it, there was a property for sale in West Street, which leads from Corfe's Market Square to the Common. Here were many thatched cottages, but this house dated from the 1930s and had 'all mod cons'.

9

Tilly Whim: Some Childhood Reminiscences

THE NEXT excursion that Rachel and I made was to Tilly Whim, a Purbeck beauty spot on the coast, and now part of Durlston Country Park. And once again the weather was clement.

This time, she wore a close-fitting dress of stretch fabric with floral decoration in tasteful, pastel colours. Her taste dictated that the colour pink must generally be included somewhere in her attire, and this time it was in the form of her leather belt. I wore a new, tartan shirt and a new pair of shorts, both of which she had chosen because, she said, she thought they suited me – not that I have one ounce of Scottish blood!

We left my Land Rover in the car park above Durlston Castle and walked down to where the cliff path began. Here, a waist-high stone wall was all that separated us from the precipitous cliffs below. We paused every so often to look down on the kittiwakes, as they flew back and forth making their characteristic cries, and at the occasional yacht as it bobbed up and down on the turquoise sea. And Rachel held on to me so tightly that I could feel her firm breast pressing against my upper arm. Finally, we reached Tilly Whim, a former cliff quarry.

As we looked down from the cliff path to a broad rocky ledge, an upturned jagged boulder caught my eye. 'I think its got some writing on it,' I said. With the aid of her binoculars, Rachel deciphered the weather-worn lettering. It read:

'Look Round
And Read
Great Nature's
Open Book'

The lighthouse at Anvil Point having come into view, we climbed to the top of the grassy slope and sat down together on the groundsheet.

We had both contributed to the picnic, Rachel with food that she had prepared herself, and I with food that I had conveniently purchased the local supermarket – which she politely declined. A figure as trim as hers, I realized, was not achieved by eating pork pies, one of which I was about to tuck into!

That evening, Rachel was in a mood to reminisce. She showed me her photograph album, with snapshots of skiing holidays, taken in the Alps with nursing friends in her pre-marital days. And here, before my eyes, was a young woman in her prime, looking windswept and slightly chubby, with fair hair that glistened and cascaded down onto her shoulders. I gathered that she was fluent in several languages, including French and German. How I would

Tilly Whim Caves by Ernest Hazlehurst, 1915.

have loved to have known her then I thought, but would we have felt the same about one another as we do now? Time is a strange phenomenon.

Suddenly, she asked me, 'Did you have a happy childhood, Andrew?'.

'Yes and no,' I replied. 'Being sent away to boarding school, which was less than a mile from our home, was no joke!

I'm so sorry,' she said. There was a pause. 'I had a very happy childhood,' said Rachel. And she proceeded to paint an idyllic picture of life at her primary school in rural Dorset, where the fields were brimful of wild flowers; the trees and hedges resonated to the sound of birdsong; and penny buns were delivered daily by the local baker for the pupils to enjoy with their bottle of milk at mid-morning break time!

She told me about May Day at her primary school in rural Dorset when she was voted the May Queen by the pupils. Whereupon, she was allowed to choose her two Maids of Honour. 'A Maypole was set up in the playground,' she said, 'and we learnt our dances, weaving back and forth and in and out, both boys and girls. And Daddy made me a May Queen's crown entwined with yellow and white flowers.'

10

Corfe Castle and a New Beginning

THE SALE of my bungalow in Poole and the purchase of the house in West Street, Corfe Castle went through without a hitch. Now I anticipated Rachel's first visit, but with some apprehension. Would she approve, I wondered, even though we had previously viewed the property together?

I scurried about searching for some clean sheets for the bed. I knew I had some somewhere. And where was the iron, for goodness sake? I eventually found it in the garage! I decided to make up both the double bed, which I normally slept in, and also the single bed in the second bedroom. Even though Rachel and I had already slept together, I did not automatically presume that she would wish to share my bed again.

Rachel duly arrived, and I was pleased to see that she looked relaxed and at ease. She seemed fascinated by one of my ornaments, a carved, wooden giraffe, black in colour, and indented with tiny white spots.

'This is nice,' she said.

'It came from Africa, from Southern Rhodesia,' I said. 'I lived there as a teenager with my parents.' But I could tell that Rachel was not primarily interested in the giraffe per se, for she ran her finger along its back and frowned. Yes, I had to admit it, dusting was not my forte!

When night-time came I was pleased to see that she had deposited her suitcase, not in the second bedroom, but in my bedroom. Not only that, she had made good use of 'her' bedside table, and also of a portion of the wardrobe! From now on, this would be *our* bedroom!

We awoke to a rainy day and decided to stay indoors. I cooked Rachel a roast: a big mistake, for I noticed that whilst politely pretending to enjoy her meal, she actually left most of it behind on the plate.

'Andrew, may I ask, from where did you source this meat?'

The truth was, that whereas I purchased the most inexpensive foodstuffs that I could find, she went in for 'free range'; 'organic'; 'corn fed', etcetera. She even took notice of 'sell by' dates!

At the lower end of West Street, where my new house was located, is Corfe's Market Square and the castle entrance. At the top end is the Common, a large area traditionally set aside for the villagers as grazing land for their cattle. Subsequently, it became the abode of ponies.

It is said that the foundations of Corfe Castle's West Street are composed of chippings of Purbeck marble down to a depth of about ten feet. The seam of marble runs between Peveril Point on the south side of Swanage Bay westwards for a distance of about 10 miles to Worbarrow Tout on the east side of Worbarrow Bay. Along this seam are quarries which have been mined since Roman times. Following the Norman Conquest in 1066, the marble was brought overland to Corfe Castle where it was 'dressed', in other words fashioned, into the slender pillars with which so many of our great churches and cathedrals are decorated.

The weather brightened so we walked up the lane to the Common and I was thrilled once again when she linked her arm in mine. Nevertheless, I found myself wondering how to entertain her. What if she became bored, and decided to take off back to Herston? But as if to read my thoughts, as she so often did, she reassured me.

'It's all right. Don't worry about me. I'm quite happy just being with you,' she said.

As for me, all was now right with the world, and the long years of loneliness, which I had endured since the divorce, were, it seemed, thankfully at an end.

11

A Home Together

TO MY great joy, Rachel accepted my invitation to come and live with me in Corfe Castle, and meanwhile, she rented out her house in Herston.

Here in Corfe we quickly established a routine. I worked on my books and gave her as much help around the house as she would permit. As she was something of a perfectionist, this was fairly minimal.

'Can I put the vacuum cleaner round for you?' I would ask.

'No, you don't go round the edges properly.'

'May I put the washing out on the line?'

'No fear! I can't trust you to hang the clothes evenly.'

I realized that, slowly but surely, Rachel was making her mark. For example, I noticed that some 'unseen hand' was gradually replacing *all* of my original clothes with new ones. I did not actually witness their disappearance in person, but noticed that first, they found their way into white plastic bags, which migrated to the conservatory, then to the garage, and from there, presumably into the charity shop or the dustbin! Meanwhile, if a new item of clothing, say a pair of trousers, was found to need shortening or taking out, out would come her sewing machine in a trice.

When I telephoned my friend, Graham to tell him that Rachel had practically taken over the running of the household, he laughed. 'It's called "Petticoat Government", Andrew,' he said.

Rachel brought over from Herston some pieces of her very best Crown Derby china and installed them in the china cabinet, 'for us to use when we have our tea together,' she said. What a step change this was from my motley collection of handle-less mugs and chipped cups and saucers!

My only bone of contention was my study. Admittedly it was a shambles, but before she tidied it up, which she did on a regular basis, as least I knew where everything was! I recalled how Thomas Hardy had banned his housekeeper from his study for the same reason – not, I hasten to add, that I regarded Rachel as my housekeeper! And how, when that good soul did finally gain admission, she had nine years of Hardy's dust and grime to cope with!

Gently, but firmly, I persuaded Rachel that her entering my study was not a good idea for either of us. But she did not give up trying, on the premise that dripping water wears away a stone.

'Are you *ever* going to dust that study of yours? I'd do it for you, but you won't let me in there!'

The resident spiders, however, were on my side.

'Ugh! I loathe them! They terrify me,' said Rachel, and I noticed that the sight of one could reduce her to a quivering jelly.

On the positive side, Rachel made good use of my oak desk, which dated from the time of the Boer War and had been gifted to me by the senior partner when I had first commenced in general practice. I had sat at that desk for eleven years as a doctor, prior to my retirement due to a back injury. When I told Rachel that, since my retirement it had become surplus to requirements, she seized upon it with glee, and it was a joy to me to see her using it to store her personal possessions; write her letters; wrap up her presents, etcetera.

In the evening we would watch TV or play Scrabble. Was it my imagination, or was I usually on the losing side? Rachel methodically recorded the scores for each game in an exercise book, and when I subsequently thumbed through it, my worst fears were confirmed. As a writer my vocabulary was probably more extensive than hers, but she was able to see the different possibilities more clearly than I.

There was no question about it! Or we simply sat together in silence, and I recalled how the famous T. E. Lawrence – Lawrence of Arabia – had once said that only when people were able to achieve this state of silent union, could they regard themselves as true friends.

In the hall was a cardboard box which I had yet to unpack, following the move. Rachel was curious as to what was in it.

'I honestly can't remember', I said. 'Why not have a look?'

Inside she found some china objects individually wrapped in newspaper.

'Oh!' she exclaimed. 'It's Hardy's Cottage!'

I had once attended pottery classes and had made a likenessof the cottage in stoneware, together with a likeness – or so I hoped! – of Hardy sitting on a seat.

'Shall we put them here, on the mantlepiece,' she said, 'where they will always be in full view?'

'Where else?' I replied.

'You have made me feel alive again, after many years in the wilderness,' Rachel told me. 'You have welcomed me into your home and made me feel loved, well and truly loved, and for the very first time in my life.'

She fixed me, with that oh-so-steady gaze, and those oh-so-beautiful hazel eyes, that were that were full of tears – of joy. As for myself, I told Rachel that there was no one in the whole wide world with whom I would rather spend the rest of my life. In fact, she was the only person in the world who I would have forgiven for denting my Land Rover, which she did!

'I say, can we visit Hardy's Cottage together?' said Rachel.

'And Max Gate too, if you wish,' I replied.

12

A Visit to the Very Heart of 'Hardy Country'

TO CENTRAL southern England and the West of England, Hardy gave the name 'Wessex', after a medieval Anglo-Saxon kingdom of that name. It is true that every part of what Hardy called 'Wessex' may be regarded, to a greater or lesser extent, as 'Hardy Country' but his birthplace at Higher Bockhampton near Dorset's county town Dorchester, has a special significance.

Here, Hardy listened to stories, told to him at his mother, Jemima's knee. In the surrounding heathland, which became 'Egdon Heath', he absorbed the atmosphere as no other: daydreamed; and conjured up heroes, heroines, and villains, who would feature in works to come. In his bedroom, beneath the thatched roof, he wrote poetry, including 'Domicilium', composed at the age of sixteen.

Rachel espied a framed copy of the poem hanging on the wall of Hardy's Cottage. Whereupon, she read aloud the first verse:

> 'It faces west, and round the back and sides
> High beeches, bending, hang a veil of boughs,
> And sweep against the roof. Wild honeysucks

Climb on the walls and seem to sprout a wish
(If we may fancy wish of trees and plants)
To overtop the apple trees hard-by.'

*Hardy's
Cottage, Higher
Bockhampton,
Dorchester. The
National Trust.*

It was here that Hardy completed his first published novel, *Desperate Remedies*.

After a visit to a local hostelry for a Dorset cream tea it was on to nearby Max Gate, where Hardy lived with his first wife, Emma and after her death, with his second wife, Florence. It was here that he wrote five novels including *Jude the Obscure* and eight collections of poetry, and many short stories. And in the summer of 1923, when he was in his eighty-third year and famous, Hardy entertained to luncheon no less a person than the Prince of Wales – later King Edward VIII!

*Max Gate, Dorchester.
Andrew Leah.*

13

My Books: Rachel gets Personally Involved with Thomas Hardy

ONE DAY, Rachel asked me if I regarded the writing of my books as the most important part of my life, more important to me than she herself was. Can she be serious, I asked myself, or was she craftily fishing for compliments?

'Writing is important to me, yes,' I admitted. 'But you must remember that after my back injury my role in life was taken away from me.' The truth was, however, that Rachel too had become an integral part of my life, and I simply could not imagine life without her.

Rachel asked if she might read the manuscript that I was currently working on: a biography. And when I agreed, she sat up reading it late into the night. Next day, when I returned to it, I discovered, to my amazement, that she had proofread the entire work, making the necessary corrections in pencil. She had also made a number of helpful suggestions in the margins, as to how the narrative might be improved, and how it might be concluded, all of which I took on board. The onlooker often sees more of the game, I thought ruefully. But then I remembered her telling me that she had once done proofreading for a living.

I had another reason to be grateful to Rachel. When she saw that I was using (for reference) an old and battered copy of the *Oxford Dictionary* that had belonged to my parents, 'Surely we can do better than this!' she exclaimed, and before I knew it there arrived by post a brand new copy of the latest edition of the *Concise Oxford Dictionary*.

As the date of my birthday approached, I noticed that Rachel seemed to be lacking in her usual vitality. She yawned frequently, and once even fell asleep when I was holding a conversation with her. All was explained when the day dawned, and she presented me with a little square parcel. 'Careful, its delicate!' she said. It was a framed head and shoulders portrait of Thomas Hardy.

'Wow! Thank you so much!' I said, giving her a hug and a kiss. But its appearance puzzled me. It did not shine like a print, neither was it a painting. 'Did you make this yourself?'

She nodded and smiled. She told me that she had used a canvas with a very fine mesh which she had sewn in intricate cross stitch using embroidery silks.

'But how did you cope with such tiny stitching?'

'You kept asking me why I have been looking so tired recently,' she replied, 'but I could not reveal the secret. The truth is that I had to work on it late into the night in order to finish it in time for the great day.'

I hung the precious tapestry in pride of place above the mantelpiece. 'That means a great deal to me', I told her, taking her in my arms. 'In fact, more than I can ever say.'

14

An Introduction to 'Ethelberta'

THE BEACH at Studland in Purbeck has many advantages for the would-be swimmer, quite apart from the natural beauty of the bay. The sand is plentiful and of a perfect texture; the beach shelves gently; and the water quickly warms up in the sunshine.

I changed into my swimming trunks and Rachel changed into her bikini. 'Come on!' she cried, running helter-skelter into the sea and cavorting in the waves which broke first over her legs, then her abdomen, and finally her chest. I joined her and we swam together; she performed the breaststroke and I the backstroke, but not the front crawl which always seemed to aggravate my back condition.

As she swam, I swam after her, but with her skin covered in suntan lotion, she proved to be an elusive customer! To see her suntanned body and sparkling eyes, and to feel her weightless in the water, was a delight beyond words. It made me wonder what making love must be like in outer space! In this state of weightless euphoria, my backache, which was the bane of my life, disappeared as if by magic.

I left her to swim, and stretched myself out on the trusty groundsheet, the scene of so much action in the past. Then suddenly, splash! She had cupped some sea water in her hands, crept up mischievously, thrown it over me, and then run off. I chased after her, but she was too quick for me, so I lay down again but with one eye open warily in case the prank was repeated!

I collected some shells, and placed them in a circle, and when Rachel emerged from the water I asked her to stand in its centre.

'You are my *Venus Anadyomene*,' I said.

She laughed. 'I know, *Venus Rising From the Sea*, by Botticelli. How you do exaggerate, Andrew!'

'Perhaps you could indulge me by adopting the same pose as she does?'

'Whatever you say, O Master,' she replied.

'The problem is that I do not possess an enormous seashell, as in the painting,' I said, 'so these little ones will have to do.'

Old Harry Rocks by Ernest Hazlehurst, 1915.

And there she stood, with a shy smile on her face, the epitome of feminine beauty, as the sun turned the drops of water on her skin to diamonds and made her exquisite body shimmer. How lucky I am, I told myself, as I embraced her and water dripped down from her hair onto my shoulders. Forget your hairdresser, I thought. With your wet hair smarmed down on your head, to me you are even more of a beauty!

The conversation now took a more serious tone. 'Of all the characters in Hardy's novels,' I said, 'which is your favourite?'

'Ethelberta, without a doubt,' Rachel replied.

'From his eponymous novel, *The Hand of Ethelberta*?'

'In fact, by coincidence,' she said, 'that is the novel I am currently reading.'

'It's some time since I read it,' I said. 'So please remind me of the story.' In fact, this was the only one of Hardy's novels that I did not possess a copy of, even though I was familiar with the story.

'Over there to our right. See the Old Harry Rocks, at the end of Handfast Point? Ethelberta rode her donkey from Swanage along the top of Ballard Down towards the Old Harry Rocks, and then doubled back towards Nine Barrow Down and Corfe Castle.'

'Where she met Lord Mountclere,' I said. 'Yes, it's all coming back to me now.'

'To me, one of joys of the novel is that its all set right here, in Purbeck,' Rachel continued. 'In fact, Hardy came to Swanage in order to complete the work.'

15

The Hand of Ethelberta

RACHEL AND I were relaxing on sunloungers in the back garden when I fell asleep.

When I awoke, it was to find her engrossed in *The Hand of Ethelberta*, every so often pausing to feed our resident robin with breadcrumbs and some stale cake.

'May I?,' I asked her, picking up the novel.

'Of course!'

'In the Introduction, it says that Hardy commenced writing *The Hand of Ethelberta* when he was living in London with his wife, Emma not long after their honeymoon on the Continent. It was first serialized in the *Cornhill Magazine* and published in book form in 1875, when Hardy would have been in his thirty-fifth year.' I handed the book to Rachel. 'So tell me about Ethelberta.'

'Her full name was Ethelberta Chickerel,' said Rachel, and she was the daughter of a gentleman. But her father was also described as "a man in very humble circumstances". It says here at the beginning of Chapter I that:

> "she became teacher in a school, was praised by examiners, admired by gentlemen, not admired by gentlewomen, was touched up with accomplishments by masters who were coaxed into painstaking by her many graces rather than by her few coins, and, entering a mansion as governess to the daughter thereof, was stealthily married by the son."'

'Ah yes,' I said. 'The mansion was the home of Sir Ralph and Lady Pethwerwin, and Ethelberta married their son.'

'But he caught a chill on their honeymoon and sadly died,' said Rachel, 'and, not only that, Sir Ralph also died. Ethelberta was now sent to a finishing school in Bonn in Germany, and then Lady Petherwin:

> "brought the girl to England to live under her roof as daughter and companion, the condition attached being that Ethelberta was never openly to recognize her relations, for reasons which will hereafter appear."'

'Ah!,' I said. 'Class division; Hardy's favourite theme, which decreed that it was shameful for the rich to acknowledge any association with the poor!'

'What intrigues me,' I continued, 'was how Hardy and Emma came to live in Swanage, and where they actually resided when they were here.'

'That's easy,' said Rachel. 'I can tell you exactly where they lived. We could go there tomorrow and take a picnic to have on the Downs if you like.'

16

Hardy and Emma at West End Cottage

RACHEL AND I duly drove to Swanage and I parked the Land Rover on the sea front. We then walked up Seymer Road, which leads up the hill towards Durlston and the castle. Meanwhile, I had done some research into the background to Hardy's visit to the town in 1875.

Hardy first met Emma on 7 March 1870 at the Rectory, St Juliot, North Cornwall. They were both in their thirtieth year. At the time, Hardy was living in Weymouth in West Dorset, where he was employed by architect G. R. Crickmay.

Over the next four-and-a-half years, Hardy and Emma saw very little of each other, the distance from Weymouth to St Juliot being about 120 miles. However, Hardy was swept away by Emma's beauty, and they were married at St Peter's church, Paddington, on 17 September 1874 by Emma's uncle, Dr E. Hamilton Gifford, Canon of Worcester. But the fact that they had married, when they hardly knew one another was to have disastrous consequences for both of them.

The newlyweds honeymooned in France and whilst in Paris, Hardy out of curiosity and true to form, visited not one but two mortuaries with his new wife! They also visited the city of Rouen, which subsequently featured in *The Hand of Ethelberta*. On 1 October they returned home and rented rooms, first in Surbiton, South-West London, and subsequently at Westbourne Grove, West London. In respect of their visit to Swanage, it is fortunate that Emma kept a diary.

Hardy aged about thirty. Trustees of the Thomas Hardy Memorial Collection, Dorset County Museum.

Emma Lavinia Hardy (née Gifford), circa 1870, British School. Trustees of the Thomas Hardy Memorial Collection, Dorset County Museum.

Hardy and Emma arrived in Swanage on 15 July 1875 and the following day they found lodgings at West End Cottage, Belvedere Road: a cul-de-sac leading off Seymer Road on the east side of the town. The cottage was our present destination, and now there it was, before our very eyes! 'Dare we knock on the front door?', I said. 'Why not?' said Rachel.

The lady owner was not only most obliging; she was also very knowledgeable. She informed us that the Hardys' landlord and landlady were William Masters and his wife, Amelia who in 1875, were both in their forty-eighth year. She continued:

'Do you remember in *The Hand of Ethelberta*, the reference to 'the fuchsia bushes which overhung the path?' she asked. 'And do you remember the line from the novel:

> "The wind increase, and each blast raked the iron railings
> before the houses till they hummed as if in a song of
> derision?"'

West End Cottage in 2001. Jan Owens.

'Well those are the railings, just there,' and sure enough, there they were, on top of the garden's front wall.

I recalled, from reading *The Life of Thomas Hardy*, by Hardy's second wife, Florence, that Masters was an 'invalided captain of smacks and ketches'.

'West End Cottage is, and always had been, semi-detached,' continued our obliging lady owner, 'but at one time prior to the arrival of the Hardys, it was occupied by the gardener of the Royal Victoria Hotel and his family of ten children. In the gardener's time there was an internal doorway between the two cottages, which served as one house.'

'Was there room for both the Hardys and the Masters?' Rachel asked: the cottage being of only modest proportions.

'This single-storey extension on the west side is a recent addition,' said the lady. 'But look upwards and you will see a gabled first floor, set back from the main building. William Masters and his wife occupied the gabled portion of the property, which was accessed by way of a separate staircase.'

'Before you go,' said the lady owner, 'I should point out that when the Hardys were here, the front entrance was on the west side of the cottage and not at the front, as it is now.'

Swanage Bay from the Downs

We thanked her and crossed Seymer Road onto the Downs, where we had our picnic.

'So as you see,' said Rachel, 'West End cottage provided not only lodgings for the Hardys, but also the setting for Ethelberta's lodgings in Hardy's eponymous novel.'

As for myself, I could not wait to read what Hardy's wife Emma had said in her diary about the visit of herself and her husband to Swanage in the year 1875!

17

Emma Hardy's *Diary*: Swanage in the Mid-1870s

IN HER *Diary*, Emma described the scene on the eastern side of Seymer Road, known today as 'The Downs', as:

> 'An upheaved tract of land edged by cliff & shore & the ocean, in times centuries before, it had been famous marble quarries.'

As already mentioned, Peveril Point was where the marble seam began.

Another entry read:

> 'Mr A [unidentified] led her [presumably Emma] down the stone steps – telling her how this cave was more extensive than even he had full knowledge of, he had heard it had an opening on the shore, but that lately some huge pieces of rock had slipped from the cliff & almost entirely closed the entrance.'

This is probably a reference to a cliff quarry, but probably not Tilly Whim, which was only opened to the public in 1887.

In her diary entry for 7 September 1875, Emma described a trip from Swanage in the paddle steamer *Heather Bell* to the Isle of Wight, calling at Bournemouth on the way. Emma and Hardy were accompanied by Hardy's sisters, Mary and Kate who were staying with them in Swanage for a fortnight. The party would have departed from the 'Old Pier', constructed in 1859.

The *Diary* also records that on 13 September 1875, Hardy and Emma, together with Hardy's brother, Henry and his sisters, Mary and Kate 'Drove in Sommers' [sic] Van' for a 'breakfast picnic' at Corfe Castle, leaving at 7 a.m. and picking up another 15 people on the way. This was a reference to C. Summers, a Swanage carrier who advertised daily trips to Wareham by horse-drawn 'Private Omnibus' via Corfe Castle and leaving Swanage at 9 a.m. This visit paved the way for Ethelberta's expedition to Corfe, in Hardy's novel.

John Mowlem (1788-1868) by Ramsay Richard Reinagle. Swanage Museum and Heritage Centre.

On the same date, Emma wrote, 'Near Corfe, is a Manor House – Mem [memo] – to see it'. Clearly this was a reference to Encombe House, and a reminder by Emma to herself that she intended to pay it a visit.

Rachel picked up the diary and thumbed through its pages. 'Oh, look!' she said. 'Emma has illustrated her diary with little sketches of various scenes: See! Here is Captain Masters diving into the sea from his boat with just his legs sticking up in the air!'

'Which proves that Emma certainly had a sense of humour!' I said.

'And here is the *Heather Bell*, its funnel belching out smoke as it journeys from Swanage to the Isle of Wight,' she continued, 'and here is another of bathers, bathing machines, sailing boats and rowing boats on Swanage beach.' Meanwhile, Hardy himself had sketched stone being loaded from horse-drawn carts into lighters in Swanage Bay, prior to being loaded onto larger vessels at anchor in the bay.

The steamer Heather Bell *en route from Swanage to the Isle of Wight, September 1875. Sketch by Emma Hardy from her* Diary. *Dorset County Museum.*

Swanage Bay, 1875: Captain William Masters diving in for a swim from his boat. Sketch by Emma Hardy from her Diary. *Dorset County Museum.*

Hardy and Emma would have been familiar with the dozen, or so, bathing machines that were to be seen on Swanage beach in the summer months. These were roofed wooden four-wheeled carts drawn by horse and rider. The would-be swimmer would enter the machine while it was parked on the beach and change into his or her bathing costume. The costume would cover the body from the neck down to mid-thigh for the gentlemen and to lower thigh for the ladies. The machine was hauled into the sea to just a sufficient depth to allow the bather to alight by way of steps at the rear into the water. And in order that no one should suffer the embarrassment of seeing the swimmer entering the water, the machine was first turned so that the horse faced the beach!

'What landmarks would Hardy and Emma have particularly noticed during their eight-month sojourn in Swanage in the mid-1870s?' I asked Rachel.

'Why don't we go down to the sea front and see what remains,' she replied. 'And use our imaginations in respect of what used to be, but is no longer there?'

Some architectural survivals from the mid-1870s are the Royal Victoria Hotel on the seafront. This would have been clearly visible to the Hardys from West End Cottage. Likewise, the Marine Villas which were built to accommodate visitors who came to Swanage for 'health and recreation'.

Swanage beach, 1875. Bathing machines, Old Harry Rocks on right. Sketch by Emma Hardy from her Diary. *Dorset County Museum.*

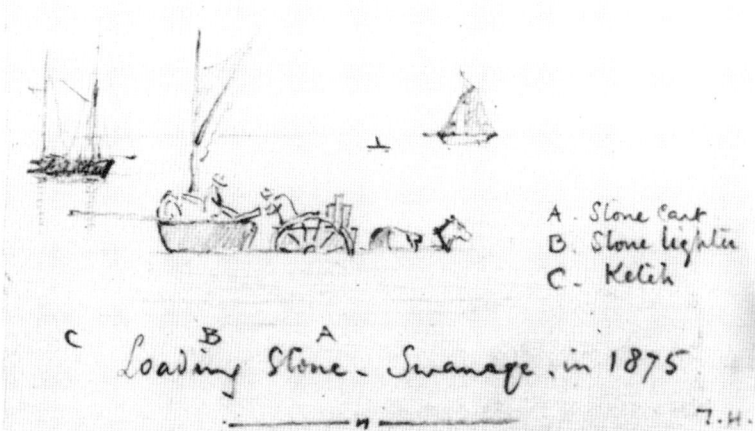

Swanage Bay, 1875: Stone being loaded into a lighter. Sketch by Thomas Hardy.
Dorset County Museum.

The place on the seafront where large amounts of stone were stored ready to be exported was known as the 'bankers'. The Swanage Pier Tramway was opened in 1858. It was designed to transport stone from the bankers to the pier, to be loaded into boats. The stone was hauled in horse-drawn carts. Today, in places, only the remains of the metal rails survive.

Swanage: the Mowlem Institute.

'Hardy would have approved of the Mowlem Institute,' I said.

'Provided by John Mowlem, the Swanage quarry boy who went to London and became a stone magnate,' said Rachel.

'And consisting of library, lecture theatre and reading room, "for the benefit and mutual improvement of the working classes",' I continued.

'Which alas no longer exists!' said Rachel.

'And here is the King Alfred Memorial,' I said,

Swanage: High Street: Purbeck House (left), Town Hall (right).

'which the Hardys could not fail to have noticed as they walked along what was then called Beach Road and is now Shore Road.' Erected in 1862 by John Mowlem, the memorial consisted of a Tuscan column set on a stepped plinth and inscribed with the following words:

'In commemoration of a great naval battle fought with the Danes in Swanage Bay by Alfred the Great. AD 877'

Mowlem died six years later, on 8 March 1868, aged seventy-nine.

Rachel pointed at the top of the memorial and laughed. 'I don't know what the eagle-eyed and sharp-brained Hardy would have made of those,' she said. She was pointing to four cannon balls, relics of the Crimean War, that had been placed atop the pillar. To the unenlightened, this gave the false impression that cannon had been used in that conflict of 877. Whereas, it was not until four centuries later that gunpowder was first used in Europe!

Swanage: The Wellington Clock Tower.

We retraced our steps until we reached the High Street where, in 1875, the year of the Hardys' arrival in Swanage, a great enterprise was under way: namely the construction (by John Mowlem's wife Susannah's nephew, George Burt, who took over the running of the London company when Mowlem retired) of an enormous mansion, Purbeck House. Built in the Scottish Baronial style, the architect was G. R. Crickmay of Weymouth, Hardy's former employer. Purbeck House is now a hotel.

'Why don't we go in and have afternoon tea?' said Rachel.

This proved to be an extraordinary experience, because inside the house, and in the garden, were artefacts brought back from London. For example, statues and busts; tiles; decorative iron panels; a gargoyle; a balustrade; the copy of a Roman pavement; an effigy of the head of Neptune in stone; and inscriptions of 'an improving nature'.

'I can imagine Burt hopping about London like a magpie,' said Rachel, 'seeking what goodies he could glean!'

Our final port of call was the Wellington Clock Tower, which overlooked the pier. 'It was originally erected at the southern

George Burt (1816-1894) by John Edgar Williams, 1879. Swanage Museum and Heritage Centre.

approach to London Bridge, but deemed to be an obstruction to traffic,' I said.

'Whereupon, George Burt, true to form, had it shipped back to Swanage!' said Rachel with a chuckle. 'No wonder Swanage was known as "Little London by the Sea!"'

'I think I know how you will be spending this evening,' I said. 'Reading *The Hand of Ethelberta*. Am I right?'

'Yes,' she replied, 'provided that you don't get your hands on it first!'

18

Swanage: Ethelberta and Hardy's 'Knollsea'

I WAS anxious to learn more about Thomas Hardy's heroine, Ethelberta and in particular, discover why Rachel considered her to be such an admirable character. The first question was, why did Ethelberta choose to relocate from London to Swanage – Hardy's 'Knollsea'?

When Ethelberta published a collection of her poems Lady Petherwin objected. Ethelberta, she said, had done this without her knowledge, and what was worse, she had not shown 'fidelity to my dear boy's memory'. In other words, to Mr Petherwin junior, Her Ladyship's son and Ethelberta's late husband. So, believing that Ethelberta had dishonoured his memory, Her Ladyship disinherited her daughter-in-law, leaving her with only the lease on a house in London.

In her London home, Ethelberta concealed her lower-class origins, and entered upper-class society as a professional storyteller, storytelling being a popular form of entertainment in mid-Victorian times.

'This is Ethelberta speaking to her sister Picotee,' said Rachel:

> 'We will have a change soon,' she said; 'we will go out of town for a few days. It will do good in many ways. I am getting so alarmed about the health of the children; their faces are becoming so white and thin and pinched that an old acquaintance would hardly

'Well, What Did You Think of My Poems?' Illustration by George Du Maurier for The Hand of Ethelberta. *Ethelberta in conversation with Picotee. Philip V. Allingham.*

know them; and they were so plump when they came. You are looking as pale as a ghost, and I daresay I am too. A week or two at Knollsea will see us right.'

"O, how charming!" said Picotee gladly.'

'Who did she mean by 'the children'?' I asked Rachel.

'Presumably her sisters: Myrtle, Georgina, and Cornelia, who she mentions later as accompanying her to Knollsea beach.'

'And why Knollsea?'

'Ethelberta chose Knollsea as her destination because of a request by her aunt,' said Rachel. 'The aunt had been born in a parish in the vicinity of Knollsea, she did not know which one, and she was anxious to discover "the secret of her birth".'

Said Ethelberta: 'Let us think of the nice little pleasure we have in store – our stay at Knollsea. There we will be as free as the wind.'

'And here is a lovely description by Hardy of the town:

"Knollsea was a seaside village lying snug within two headlands as between a finger and thumb. Everybody in the parish who was not a boatman was a quarrier, unless he were the gentleman who owned half the property and had been a quarryman, or the other gentleman who owned the other half, and had been to sea."

'As regards the first gentleman referred to,' I said, 'Hardy probably had in mind Swanage stone magnate, George Burt. As to the second, I'm not sure.'

'And here we have a description of Ethelberta in her Knollsea abode,' continued Rachel. 'Which in Hardy's imagination, was undoubtedly the real life West End Cottage.'

'Round Her, Leaning Against Branches, or Prostrate on the Ground, Were Two or Three Individuals.' Illustration by George Du Maurier for The Hand of Ethelberta. *Ethelberta rehearsing a sensational tale. Philip V. Allingham.*

'Ethelberta sat in front of a painting of a fully-rigged ship, in a light linen dress, and with tightly-knotted hair … sometimes lifting her eyes to the outlook from the window, which presented a happy combination of grange scenery with marine. Upon the irregular slope between the house and the quay was an orchard of aged trees wherein every apple ripening on the boughs presented its rubicund side towards the cottage, because that building chanced to lie upwards in the same direction as the sun.

Under the trees were a few Cape sheep, and over them the stone chimneys of the village below: outside these lay the tanned sails of a ketch or smack, and the violet waters of the bay, seamed and creased by breezes insufficient to raise waves; beyond all a curved wall of cliff, terminating in a promontory, which was flanked by tall and shining obelisks of chalk rising sheer from the trembling blue race beneath.'

19

The Adventures of Ethelberta

'WHAT ADVENTURES did Ethelberta have during her time at Knollsea?' I asked Rachel. 'I seem to remember that she visited Corfe, for example.'

'Yes, she did indeed! Prior to Ethelberta's arrival in Dorset,' said Rachel, 'both she and her sister, Picotee had attended a dinner party held by a Mr Doncastle, a friend of Lady Petherwin in his West London home. Lord Mountclere was also in attendance. Listen, Andrew! This is Picotee telling Ethelberta about His Lordship.' Rachel quickly found the relevant page, even though her edition of *The Hand of Ethelberta* was some 460 pages in length!

'And it's dreadful how fond he is of you – quite ridiculously taken up with you – I saw that well enough. Such an old man, too; I wouldn't have him for the world!'

Whereupon Lord Mountclere informed Ethelberta as follows:

'I shall be at Enckworth Court in a few days, probably at the time you are at Knollsea. The Imperial Archaeological Association holds its meetings in that part of Wessex this season, and Corvsgate Castle, near Knollsea, is one of the places on our list.'

'For "Enckworth" read Encombe House, near Kingston,' said Rachel, 'and for "Corvsgate Castle" read Corfe Castle.'

'And for the "Imperial Archaeological Association",' I said, 'read the real-life "Dorset Natural History and Antiquarian Field Club",

'So Ethelberta Went': Illustration by George Du Maurier for The Hand of Ethelberta. *Ethelberta on her way from Knollsea to Corvesgate.*

which was founded in 1875, the very year that Hardy and Emma came to Swanage, in fact.'

Lord Mountclere, said that he hoped that Ethelberta would be able to attend, Rachel continued, as this would be 'a desirable and exhilarating change after her laborious season's work in town.' Whereupon, Ethelberta asked Picotee:

> 'Did you ever hear anything so strange? Now, I should like to attend very much, not on Lord Mountclere's account, but because such gatherings are interesting, and I have never been to one; yet there is this to be considered, would it be right for me to go without a friend to such a place?'

'And did Ethelberta accept Lord Mountclere's invitation?' I asked.

'Yes, she did,' replied Rachel. 'But the question now was, how was she to get to what Hardy described as "the celebrated ruin", which was "not more than five miles" distant?'

'By "celebrated ruin", I take it Hardy meant the castle,' I said, 'or did he mean Lord Mountclere?' and we both laughed.

Ethelberta finally decided, said Rachel, that:

> 'It would be inconsiderate to the children to spend a pound on a brougham when as much as she could spare was wanted for their holiday. It was almost too far to walk. She had, however, decided to walk, when she met a boy with a donkey who offered to lend it to her for three shillings. The animal was rather sad-looking, but Ethelberta found she could sit upon the pad without discomfort.'

'Brougham: a carriage pulled by a single horse,' I interrupted. 'As for "pad", presumably that means saddle.'

> 'Considering that she might pull up some distance short of the castle and leave the ass at a cottage before joining her four-wheeled friends, she struck the bargain and rode on her way.'

'In other words, it would not do for the assembled company to see that Ethelberta was so poor that she could not afford to hire a horse-drawn carriage,' I said. 'And that is presumably why she chose to take a route over the hills, rather than along the main road, which would have been less arduous and more direct, again so as not to risk being seen.'

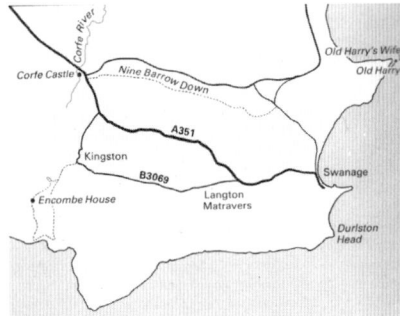

Ethelberta's route from Swanage ('Knollsea') to Corfe Castle ('Corvesgate') by way of Nine Barrow Down. Hermann Lea: The Hardy Guides.

'Do look at this, Andrew,' said Rachel, and she pointed to one of artist Andrew du Maurier's 17 illustrations for *The Hand of Ethelberta*. Ethelberta was depicted riding side-saddle on her donkey, but Ballard Down was to her *left*.

'He's got her travelling in the opposite direction,' I said. 'What a mistake to make!'

Rachel's eyes suddenly lit up. 'What say we follow in Ethelberta's footsteps?' she said.

'What, trudge all the way from Swanage to Corfe? You must be joking!' I studied the Ordnance Survey map. The total distance from West End Cottage, Belvedere Road, to Corfe Castle, assuming we took the route across the hills as Ethelberta had done, was 6½ miles!

Yes, I thought, we could both just about manage that, provided that I took painkillers for my back, and provided that Rachel was not having one of her attacks of fibromyalgia. I found myself relishing the prospect of another excursion into the fabulous Dorset countryside with my beloved Rachel, the love of my life, who had given me a new lease of life!

Corfe Castle from Nine Barrow Down, 1906, by Walter Tyndale.

20

Nine Barrow Down:
Here We Come!

WE SET off on foot one bright day, beginning at West End Cottage and faithfully retracing Ethelberta's footsteps from there. First there was a short descent down Seymer Road to the High Street; a left turn and then a right into Institute Road, and straight on to Shore Road and the promenade, which follows the sweep of the bay.

'One day, after a storm,' I told Rachel, 'I found the bowl of a clay pipe lying amidst some pebbles here on the beach.'

'It may have dated from Hardy's time,' she said.

Ethelberta had travelled by donkey, and elderly residents of Swanage still remembered times when donkey rides were on offer on Swanage beach.

Rachel had brought her copy of *The Hand of Ethelberta* with her and she read aloud the various passages at the appropriate places on the journey, in order that we could relive Ethelberta's adventure vicariously with the aid of Hardy's description. She travelled:

> 'First by a path on the shore where the tide dragged huskily up and down the shingle without disturbing it, and thence up the steep crest of land opposite, whereon she lingered awhile to let the ass breathe.'

The 'steep crest' was a reference to Ballard Down, 530 feet above sea level, which we now ascended.

'Dear little donkey,' said Rachel when we reached the top of the ridge, breathless and desperate for a refreshing cup of coffee from our flask. 'I wish we had two of his kind with us now.'

'I second that,' I said, and began to wonder if we had taken on too much.

The scene was just as Hardy had described it. We were standing on what he called 'the thumb', of the finger and thumb between which lay Swanage Bay. In the distance, we could see Peveril Point, the 'finger'.

In the opposite direction, to the north, a vast expanse of heathland was visible with Poole Harbour and its islands in the distance. As for our companions, there were few humans beings to be seen that day, but many sheep, cows, and rabbits!

Now came a passage from *The Hand of Ethelberta* that surprised us:

'On one of the spires of chalk into which the hill here had been split was perched a cormorant, silent and motionless, with wings spread out to dry in the sun after his morning's fishing, their white surface shining like mail.'

'One of the spires' was a clear reference to the stack rocks at the end of Handfast Point, where the Purbeck Hills terminated at their most easterly point. The largest of the stacks was affectionately known as 'Old Harry', after a notorious Poole pirate; and a smaller one as 'Old Harry's Wife'. And 'mail' was clearly a reference to armour.

'But surely Andrew, the direct way would have been for Ethelberta to have turned *left* at the summit of Ballard Down,' said Rachel. 'Not *right*, towards Old Harry?'

I consulted the map and discovered that such a detour would have added another 4 miles at least to Ethelberta's journey, 2 miles there and 2 miles back. 'A bit of poetic licence on Hardy's part, I think, Rachel,' I said.

She continued to read from the novel:

Corfe Castle from West Street, 1906, by Walter Tyndale.

'Retiring without disturbing him – the cormorant, that is – and turning to the left along the lofty ridge which ran inland, the country on each side lay beneath her like a map, domains behind domains, parishes by the score, harbours, fir-woods, and little inland seas mixing curiously together.'

The most significant of these 'inland seas' was, of course, Poole Harbour. We descended to Ulwell, crossed the main road, and ascended Godlingston Hill. Here, there are two Bronze Age prehistoric barrows named 'The Giant's Grave' and 'The Giant's Trencher', but we found them to be overgrown with vegetation.

Rachel continued:

'Thence she ambled along through a huge cemetery of barrows, containing human dust from prehistoric times.'

This was a reference to Nine Barrow Down, 650 feet above sea level where, according to historian, Rodney Legg there are, in fact, 17 barrows:

> 'set in a line running for 800 feet along the crest of the Purbeck ridge. The largest is 100 feet in diameter and ten feet high, surrounded by a substantial ditch'.

And here they were, in the shape of rounded mounds, before our very eyes! The barrows dated from between 2100 BCE and 1500 BCE, which is the Middle period of the Bronze Age.

Furthermore, at the eastern end of these barrows 'is an earlier Neolithic long barrow 112 feet long by 40 feet wide' which 'would have been built to cover collective burials of about 3500 BCE in the Late Stone Age.'

We continued westward to Allwood Down, Brenscombe Hill, and Rollington Hill. Finally, we skirted around the south side of Challow Hill, when suddenly, Corfe Castle came into view, perched as it is on a mound in a gap in the ridge of Purbeck Hills.

Rachel now read aloud from the novel once again:

> 'The towers of the notable ruin to be visited rose out of the furthermost shoulder of the upland as she [Elfrida] advanced, its site being the slope and crest of a smoothly nibbled mount at the toe of the ridge she had followed.'

Hardy was an indefatigable explorer who had travelled the length and breadth of Dorset on his bicycle. In later life he travelled by motor car, driven by chauffeur Harold Voss. There is little doubt, therefore, that he had witnessed this scene with his very eyes.

21

Corfe Castle: Dorset's 'Jewel in the Crown'

WE GAZED in wonder at the sight before us. The little village of Corfe with its church of St Edward King and Martyr – the tower of which was clearly visible and the castle.

Even though Corfe Castle was slighted by the Parliamentarians after its capture during the English Civil War, it remains a truly remarkable sight; perhaps even more impressive in its present ruined state than it had been when new: more evocative, certainly. For this was, without doubt, Dorset's most iconic landmark.

We paused for a while and I spread the groundsheet out beside the pathway and we both flopped down on it, glad to take a breather after our exertions.

'How is your back, Andrew?' asked Rachel.

'Its fine,' I replied, when in fact it was hurting like hell! But being able to share these precious moments with her more than made up for it.

From our vantage point high above, the features of the castle were clearly visible. The outer defensive so-called 'curtain wall', which surrounded the entire structure; the great ditch; the bridge leading to the outer gatehouse, which guarded the outer 'ward', or separately defensible area; the inner gatehouse – equally impressive, which guarded the second ward, and finally, the great keep.

Corfe Castle's keep projects 70 feet into the sky from the summit of the mound on which it stands. On a clear day it is

Corfe Castle and South-East Purbeck. Ordnance Survey, 1895.

visible from as far away as Poole Quay, 6 miles away to the east as the crow flies.

We drank the last of our coffee and I made Rachel a 'daisy chain' bracelet. We then fell to discussing Thomas Hardy. After all, he was the reason for our presence here today.

'Would you call him a pessimist?' Rachel asked me.

'In my opinion,' I replied, 'those who call Hardy a pessimist without any further qualification have not studied novels like *Under the Greenwood Tree* and *The Woodlanders*, which are full of wit, humour, and jollity.'

'But what of his later works?'

'There's no doubt that with the passage of time, Hardy became more and more melancholic, and this melancholia was reflected in his later works.'

'So how would you describe him?' asked Rachel.

'He was more of a fatalist than a pessimist, I would say,' I replied. 'I was thinking of his historical narrative, *The Dynasts*.'

'Ah yes, where he refers to the "Urging Immanence", a kind of supernatural force which controls all our destinies.'

'Add this fatalism to the two other elements which in his view were designed to ensure the continued misery of the so-called working classes, namely religious convention and the class system, and it was no wonder that Hardy was depressed at times!'

'But he railed against what he considered to be these two evils, not only in his novels, but also in other ways', said Rachel. 'Take his pamphlet entitled "The Dorset Farm Labourer", for example, where he champions the poor and the oppressed.'

'Why did he become such a misery, do you suppose?' asked Rachel, 'and write such heartbreaking stuff?'

'Culminating in *Jude the Obscure*,' I replied. Yes, I know exactly what you mean. In my opinion it had to do with his unfortunate marriage.'

'To his first wife, Emma you mean, whom he met as a young architect when sent on an assignment to Cornwall and returned with "magic" in his eyes?'

As Rachel spoke, the sun lit up her face. She looked lovelier than ever, and I knew instantly, why Hardy had used the word 'magic'.

'So, he fell in love with this beautiful apparition,' she continued, 'And then what?'

'He found that he and she were emotionally and intellectually completely incompatible, so much so that in Emma's later years, he and she lived separate lives under the same roof.'

'It's strange though,' said Rachel, 'that when Emma died, Hardy was filled with remorse.'

'Certainly. He wrote dozens and dozens of poems in her memory and dragged Florence, his second wife, on a nostalgic journey – for him but not for her! – to all the places that he had visited with his late wife!'

'Poor, long-suffering Florence,' said Rachel.

'Could Hardy have written so poignantly and with such depth of feeling had he not suffered so?' Rachel asked.

We stood up and I gave her a long hug. 'Heaven forbid that I should ever lose my beloved Rachel!' I thought. Then I shivered involuntarily and hoped that she would not notice.

It had been a long day, so we caught the open-top bus back to Swanage. Our in-depth examination of the castle and the opportunity to compare our experience with that of Ethelberta, would have to wait for another day.

22

Ethelberta and 'Corvsgate Castle'

HARDY'S NAME for Corfe's castle was originally 'Coombe Castle', but he subsequently changed it to 'Corvsgate Castle'.

In anticipation of our visit to the castle, which is owned by the National Trust, Rachel said she could not wait to view it vicariously through the character of Ethelberta. And as we only possessed one copy of the novel, I was impatient for her to bring me up to date.

'We had left Hardy's heroine within sight of the ancient ruin, if you remember,' said Rachel. 'Now she has convinced herself that the meeting of the Imperial Archaeological Association will not take place, owing to the inclement weather, so she decides to ride her donkey right into the castle grounds.'

'Accordingly, Ethelberta crossed the bridge over the moat, and rode under the first archway into the outer ward. As she had expected, not a soul was here. The arrow-slits, portcullis-grooves, and staircases met her eye as familiar friends, for in her childhood she had once paid a visit to the spot. Ascending the green incline and through another arch into the second ward, she still pressed on, till at last the ass was unable to clamber an inch further. Here she dismounted and tying him to a stone which projected like a fang from a raw edge of wall, performed the remainder of the ascent on foot. Once among the towers above, she became so interested in the windy corridors, mildewed dungeons, and the tribe of daws [presumably jackdaws] peering invidiously upon her from overhead, that she forgot the flight of time.'

Our appetite having been duly whetted, Rachel and I set off down West Street towards the castle, taking the precious novel on which our future movements seemed increasingly to depend, with us!

On arrival, we observed in the outer gatehouse the very arrow slits as described above, and also the groove into which the portcullis had once fitted. And here were the aforementioned staircases, both within the great gatehouses and also at intervals in the walls, to allow the defenders to climb up to the walkways near the top. And there were many jackdaws to be seen, long-time residents of this ancient place.

Corfe Castle: the Model Village. Ed Paris.

The construction of Corfe Castle's mighty keep was ordered by King Henry I in the twelfth century. Prior to this a timber structure existed on the site. The castle is famous for many reasons, but especially for the fact that Lady Bankes, wife of Sir John Bankes, Chief Justice at the Court of Common Pleas, defended it with a few faithful followers during its siege by the Parliamentarians between 1643 and 1645. Her Ladyship was finally betrayed by one of the castle's defenders.

During the Civil War, the Parliamentarians or 'rebels' had no respect for Corfe's nearby church of St Edward King and Martyr. They stabled their horses inside the building and used the font as a drinking trough for the animals. Out of the surplices, the white linen vestments worn over their cassocks by the clergy, the rebels made shirts for their soldiers. They broke up the organ and used the pipes to hold their powder and shot and they cut the lead off the church roof in order to make bullets for their muskets.

'What happens next in the story,' said Rachel, 'is that Lord Mountclere appears and Ethelberta estimates his age to be "about sixty-five". From a distance, he had a "dignified aspect", but on closer inspection, she observed a "jocund slyness".'

'What about the donkey?' I asked.

'His Lordship noticed it, but Ethelberta, fearful of being held up to ridicule, disowned the poor creature, and "gazed at her untoward beast as if she had never before beheld him".'

'In the event,' Rachel continued, 'the meeting did take place, and a Dr Yore duly "read the paper on the castle", "tracing its development from a mound with a few earthworks … to the final overthrow of the stern old pile" by the Parliamentarians in 1645'.

'Some of Lord Mountclere's party, including himself and Ethelberta, wandered now into a cool dungeon, partly open to the air overhead, where long arms of ivy hung between their eyes and the white sky.'

'That's what we've just been looking at!' I exclaimed. 'The windowless, sunken room in the inner ward. It could only have been a dungeon! The French call it an "oubliette" – from "oublier" – to forget, as many captured French knights who were imprisoned here and left to starve to death, learned to their cost!'

No visit to Corfe Castle is complete without viewing the model village, built to a scale 1/20, in which the castle appears as it was prior to the Civil War, and before it was deliberately wrecked by Oliver Cromwell's men. Each building was handmade by Parkstone builder, Jack Phillips; the roof tiles being made from tiny fragments of Purbeck stone. The project took two years, and the opening day was 7 April 1966.

23

Corfe Castle: Hardy's 'Corvsgate'

I FELT like a little boy again, waiting for my mother to tell me a story. But this was not my late mother, it was Rachel, the new found love of my life.

I found myself itching for Rachel to tell me into what fresh fields and pastures new Ethelberta ventured next, always provided that it was in Purbeck, of course! But I was disappointed to learn that it was to France that she next journeyed.

'Before Ethelberta returned home on her faithful donkey,' said Rachel, 'she was informed that Lord Mountclere and his party would probably be paying a visit to Knollsea. Whereupon, she decided to visit her aunt in Normandy. She would travel on the "little pleasure steamer" which "crossed to Cherbourg once a week during the summer" and travel from there onwards to Rouen.'

'Where Hardy spent part of his honeymoon,' I said.

'On Monday morning,' Rachel continued, 'the little steamer, *Speedwell,* made her appearance round the promontory by Knollsea Bay, to take in passengers for the transit to Cherbourg. They – that is Ethelberta and her sister, Cornelia – "left the pier at eight o'clock taking at first a short easterly course to avoid a sinister ledge of limestones jutting from the water like crocodile's teeth, which first obtained notoriety in English history through being the spot whereon a formidable Danish fleet went to pieces a thousand years ago".'

The 'sinister ledge' is a rock formation that stretches eastward from Peveril Point on the north side of Swanage Bay – the so-called Peveril Ledge. For one-third of a mile out to sea, the rocks themselves were a hazard to shipping, and not only that, ships could be swept onto the ledge by the tidal race, which ran across both the ledge and for a further half-a-mile beyond it. Many vessels had come to grief here, and it was no coincidence that the Swanage Lifeboat station was situated close by.

'So, what did Lord Mountclere do? He followed Ethelberta to Cherbourg in his yacht *Fawn*', said Rachel. 'And furthermore, he made a point of catching the same train to Rouen as she did! Finally, he attempted to extract from Ethelberta a promise that she would marry him!'

24

A New Residence for Ethelberta

WHEN RACHEL went to Bournemouth to do some shopping I became impatient, so instead of waiting for her to return and give me the next instalment of Ethelberta's life, I took the initiative, borrowed her copy of the novel, and read it for myself. The outcome was this:

On her return to Knollsea, Ethelberta heard from Lord Mountclere that he proposed to call on her. Not wishing for him to see her in her modest West End Cottage, she told Picotee that they must seek more upmarket accommodation, and 'look for the gayest house we can find.'

> 'She found no difficulty in arranging for a red and yellow streaked villa, which was so bright and glowing that the sun seemed to be shining upon it even on a cloudy day, and the ruddiest native looked pale when standing by its walls. It was not without regret that she renounced the sailor's pretty cottage for this porticoed and balconied dwelling; but her lines were laid down clearly at last, and thither she removed forthwith.'

Furthermore, said Ethelberta, they had relocated to this 'variagated brick and stone villa … in order to be in keeping with their ascending fortunes.' Was this villa an invention of Hardy's, I wondered, or did it exist in reality?

Hermann Lea collaborated with Hardy to document the places immortalized in the great novelist's works. According to Lea, the

Durlston Cottage, 1926 by Professor R. W. Pickford. British Listed Buildings.

house to which Ethelberta relocated was subsequently 'altered to a more modern structure' and renamed 'Durlston Cottage'.

A watercolour painting exists, dated 1926 but unsigned, of Durlston Cottage in which the rendered walls were of a reddish-brown colour. Also, a photograph exists of the cottage, taken in 1958, in which the outside walls are cream in colour. But, in neither the painting nor the photograph are there porticoes or balconies.

According to an inventory of historic buildings, Durlston Cottage is described as having:

> 'Two storeys, rendered walls, low-pitched slate roof, two
> canted [oblique] bay windows on each floor, with double-
> hung sashes. Central doorway with semi-circular head
> and fanlight.'

It is also recorded that this was once the home of a lime buyer, who burnt lime in order to produce quicklime, which was used to make limewash – a mixture of lime and water used for coating walls.

Did this cottage still exist? With some difficulty, Rachel and I discovered it at the top end of Seymer Road, tucked away in a spinney. 'Just look at all the daffodils and primroses!' she said. There were drifts of them; in the lush grass; on the lawns, on the banks, and at the foot of the trees. And suddenly, there it was, its front façade exactly as depicted in the both the watercolour and the photograph.

The cottage faces north and at the time of the Hardys' visit its occupants would have enjoyed fabulous views of Swanage Bay and the Purbeck Hills beyond. Now, however, trees completely obscured the view.

I estimated that this property was about double the size of West End Cottage and would therefore have provided Ethelberta and her family a much more adequate living space.

The owner kindly let us view the back garden, where there was a raised terrace laid down to lawn. Beyond this were the lime kilns, now overgrown with ivy. The fumes given off when lime is burnt are toxic, and this may explain why the cottage originally stood some distance away from other properties.

This then, was where Ethelberta relocated to from West End Cottage, and before the trees grew up around it, it had provided as fine an uninterrupted view of Swanage Bay as any property in the town.

While Ethelberta was awaiting the arrival of Lord Mountclere she heard a noise, which Picotee said was 'the fizz of a rocket. The coastguardsmen are practising the life apparatus today, to be ready for the autumn wrecks.' At the time in which the story is set there was a coastguard station at Peveril Point and when a ship became stranded on the Peveril Ledge, the local coastguards would fire a rocket carrying a rope to it. Whereupon, the shipwrecked sailors would make the rope fast to their ship and shin along it to the shore.

Lord Mountclere was unable to keep his appointment with Ethelberta owing to an accident. Having explained this to her, he expressed the desire that 'she would come to Lychworth Court and delight himself and a small group of friends who were visiting there.'

'"Lychworth Court" was Hardy's name for Encombe House near Kingston – which he called "Little Lychworth". Am I right?' I asked Rachel, even though I already knew the answer.

'You've been cheating!' she said. 'You've been reading my book!' We had now reached page 295 of this epic tale!

Durlston Cottage, 2021. Harry Thorpe.

25

A Visit to Encombe House: Hardy's 'Lychworth Court'

RACHEL KINDLY agreed to relax her proprietorial grip on *The Hand of Ethelberta* – fair enough, it was her copy after all! – so when the time came for our visit to Encombe, we were both fully 'genned up'. Not only that, I had done my homework in respect of the real life history of the great house. By now Rachel, like me, had well and truly caught the bug! 'When can we go? Can we go tomorrow?' she said.

Following in Ethelberta's footsteps we drove the 4 miles east from Swanage to Encombe: first ascending the long hill to Langton Matravers and then carrying on, along the high road. From here, in the distance, Corfe Castle could be seen, nestling in the cleft in the Purbeck Hills known as 'Corfe Gap'.

At the little hamlet of Kingston, we took a left turn. Here, on the corner, was the 'Scott Arms' public house, and a mile or so beyond, on our left, was the magical sign, 'ENCOMBE'!

The road wound tortuously down into a thickly wooded valley with ever steeper sides. On the banks were clumps of brilliant yellow daffodils and primroses. Shafts of sunlight created a dappling effect, and brought to mind the poem by Gerald Manley Hopkins, 'Glory be to God for dappled things'. We had found another 'Garden of Eden'. How lucky we are, I thought, to be pursuing a hobby which we both enjoyed.

When we came to a sign saying 'PRIVATE', I turned the Land Rover round and drove back to the car park. A short walk through

Kingston ('Little Lychworth') with a distant view of Corfe Castle, 1907,
by John W. G. Bond.

a wood brought us to open country on the east side of the Encombe Valley. 'Oh look,' said the eagle-eyed Rachel. 'I can see two hares boxing in that field over there!'

After a while, Encombe House, or 'Lychworth Court', as Hardy called it, came into view and from our vantage point we had, in effect, an aerial view, not only of the house itself, but also of the adjacent lake and the walled vegetable garden.

Hardy was a qualified architect and I was interested to read what he had to say about the house. 'Lychworth Court, in its main part,' he said, 'had not been standing more than a hundred years.' And yet, when the house had been enlarged, there was not 'perfect harmony' between the old part and the new.

Rachel now took up the novel:

'When the vast addition had just been completed, King George visited Enckworth. Its owner pointed out the features of its grand architectural attempt, and waited for commendation.

"Brick, brick, brick," said the king.'

89

'The outcome was,' Rachel continued, 'that, seeing the monarch's objection to brick, Lord Mountclere, at great expense to himself, immediately took drastic action.'

> 'Thin freestone slabs were affixed to the whole series of fronts by copper cramps and dowels, each one of substance sufficient to have furnished a poor boy's pocket with pennies for a month, till not a speck of the original surface remained.'

The truth was, however, that in respect of Encombe House, Hardy's account was a mixture of fact and fiction.

In 1735, John Pitt, 1st Earl of Chatham inherited the Encombe estate. He was an amateur architect and as such, designed a new house, incorporating into it elements of the existing building. Pitt's new house was completed in about 1770. So yes, Hardy was correct in stating that at the time in question, the house was about a century old. But the building was faced with ashlar – finely cut and dressed stone, *not* brick. So where had Hardy got the idea about the king's visit from? I believe that it was Kingston Maurward, a Georgian country house near Dorset's county town of Dorchester, that Hardy had in mind. The house was built in red brick, but after derogatory comments about this by King George III, its owner, William Morton Pitt had it clad entirely in Portland limestone!

As for the real life Encombe House, Pitt created an extensive park with picturesque grotto; a lake on the south side of the house, and a circuit of carriage drives.

Finally, in about 1870 and five years prior to the Hardys' visit to Swanage in 1875, John Scott, 3rd Earl of Eldon and Encombe's current owner, had the house remodelled.

'So "on a dull, stagnant, noiseless afternoon of autumn",' said Rachel, '"Ethelberta first crossed the threshold of Lychworth Court".'

'Furthermore,' I said, 'Hardy described her thus, as a great beauty:

Encombe House ('Lychworth House').

> "Ethelberta, in a dress sloped about as high over the shoulder as would have drawn approval from Reynolds, and expostulation from Lely."'

'Which was undoubtedly why Lord Mountclere was attracted to her,' said Rachel. 'And furthermore Ethelberta had immense charm. She:

> "thawed and thawed each friend who came near her and sent him or her away smiling."'

'That evening the assembled company, knowing that Ethelberta was a professional storyteller, prevailed upon her to tell them a story. And when she did, it was about "a girl of the poorest and meanest parentage" who had become a nursery governess and teacher, had married the son of the house, and shortly afterwards become a widow.'

But then, Ethelberta spoke in the first-person, saying, 'I thus was reduced to great distress, and vainly cast about me for directions what to do.' She then broke down, realising that she had given the game away, and that both Lord Mountclere and her audience now knew the truth about her humble ancestry, and that this would prove 'fatal to all her matrimonial ambitions.'

'But as we know,' I said, 'Ethelberta need not have worried, because Lord Mountclere came up trumps. He confessed that he had already known of Ethelberta's humble origins, even before he had made his first proposal of marriage. And he now repeated his proposal, to which she replied, "I shall think it a great honour to be your wife".'

'Well good for His Lordship!' said Rachel, and she gave me a knowing look.

26

Sol Chickerel and the Hon. Edgar Mountclere Attempt to Prevent the Marriage

ETHELBERTA'S BROTHER Sol Chickerel, and Lord Mountclere's brother, the Honourable Edgar Mountclere were both opposed to Ethelberta's marriage to Lord Mountclere, but for different reasons.

Said Sol, 'I would lose a winter's work to prevent her marrying him. What does she want to go mixing with people who despise her for?' As for the Hon. Edgar, his opposition was based on the notion that 'my brother is evidently ignorant of the position of Mrs Petherwin's family and connections.' But as already mentioned, this was not in fact, the case. As for Ethelberta's father, 'Her marriage with Lord Mountclere means misery,' he declared.

The outcome was that Sol and Edgar caught the steamer *Spruce* from Sandbourne (Bournemouth) and sailed for Knollsea (Swanage). However, a strong easterly wind threatened to blow them onto the Old Harry Rocks, and when they reached Knollsea, they were told that the pier had been damaged in the gale. It was, therefore, unsafe for them to effect a landing and they were obliged to turn back.

The pier, said Hardy in the novel:

'consisted simply of a row of rotten piles covered with rotten planking, no balustrade of any kind existing to keep the unwary from tumbling off. At the water level the piles were eaten away by the action of the sea to about the size of a man's wrist, and at every fresh influx the whole structure trembled like a spider's web.'

Hardy himself, described just how ominous the sea could sound in the vicinity of Swanage when a gale blew up:

'Evening. Just after sunset. Sitting with E. [his wife Emma] on a stone under the wall before the Refreshment Cottage. The sounds are two, and only two. On the left Durlston Head [Hardy spelt it 'Durlstone' with an 'e'] roaring high and low, like a giant asleep. On the right a thrush. Above the bird hangs the new moon, and a steady planet.'

Undeterred, Sol and Edgar travelled by horse and carriage to Anglebury (Wareham) where they visited the 'Old Fox' inn (one of Hardy's names for the 'Red Lion'). Roughly halfway between Bournemouth and Swanage, this was a convenient place for travellers to refresh themselves and have a change of horses. But when they arrived at Lychworth Court, it was to find that Lord Mountclere had already left.

'Sorry, but the suspense is killing me!' said Rachel, taking the book from my hands. 'Did they get married in time, or did they not? Ah, here we are! Sol and Edgar journeyed on to Knollsea, and en route they were joined by Ethelberta's father, Mr Chickerel'.

'In about twenty minutes the square unembattled tower of Knollsea Church appeared below them in the vale, its summit just touching the distant line of sea upon sky. They descended the road to the village at a little more mannerly pace than that of the earlier journey and saw the rays glance upon the hands of the church clock, which marked five-and-twenty minutes to nine.'

'All Before Them Was A Sheet of Whiteness.' Illustration by George Du Maurier for The Hand of Ethelberta. *On the seafront at Knollsea.*

However, they were too late. The wedding had already taken place and the couple had already signed the marriage register and departed.

Not to be outdone, Rachel and I caught the pleasure boat from Swanage Pier, in the hope of seeing guillemots and dolphins. The skipper gave the wicked Peveril Ledge a wide berth and we crossed Durlston Bay to Durlston Head, where Durlston Castle loomed above us. And as we rounded the head, the 'Great Globe' came in sight. This is a huge stone sphere representing the Earth.

And there were the guillemots – miniature penguins in black and white plumage – huddled together on a rocky ledge one-third of the way up the cliff and 40 feet above the waves.

'I've read up about guillemots,' said Rachel, studying them through her binoculars as the little boat bobbed up and down. 'When the time is right, the young ones leap from the ledge into the sea, where their father spends about a fortnight teaching them to fish. Then they leave for the deep ocean and return five years later as adults in order to breed.'

27

The Admirable Ethelberta!

ALTHOUGH *THE Hand of Ethelberta* is considered by some not to be amongst the finest of Hardy's novels, Rachel and I agreed that we absolutely loved it. 'Why do you think that is?' I asked. 'Hardy put it best,' she replied, 'when he pointed out in the Preface that this was a novel:

> "Wherein servants were as important as, or more important than, their masters; wherein the drawing-room was sketched in many cases from the point of the servants' hall."'

As regards the heroine Ethelberta, the light was beginning to dawn on me as to why Rachel considered her to be such an admirable character in every way. After all, she became a successful and published poet and carved out a career for herself as a professional storyteller. At her London home, she made a point of helping the impoverished members of her family by employing them as her servants. Although she had three admirers – the struggling musician Christopher Julian; two gentlemen, Mr Neigh and Mr Ladywell; and finally Lord Mountclere – her main concern was to marry one of sufficient wealth as would enable her to continue to support her family – which she did.

Furthermore, Ethelberta had agreed to marry Lord Mountclere only if he would do his utmost 'to ensure a marriage' between her sister and her former admirer, Christopher Julian, whom Picotee loved. This, His Lordship did by promising Christopher, who by his own admission was 'as poor as Job', the sum of five hundred pounds when they married.

'What of the novel itself?' Rachel enquired. 'Is it not unusual for Hardy,' she said with a laugh, 'to have not one single suicide, only one tragic death, and a happy ending?'

My reaction to this was as follows: *The Hand of Ethelberta* was Hardy's fifth published novel. He composed it around the time of his marriage to Emma when he was deeply in love. The subtitle of the novel is 'A Comedy in Chapters', and he was in a happy and humorous frame of mind when he wrote it. Alas, in his marriage, this would not always be the case.

Hardy completed *The Hand of Ethelberta* in January 1876 and sent the manuscript to the publisher Smith, Elder & Co.

Finally, it is no coincidence that the title page of the novel carried the motto, 'Vitae post scenia celant', a quote from Lucretius, which may be translated to read, 'They hide behind the scenes of life'. In fact, in *The Hand of Ethelberta*, Hardy had *raised* the curtain on life behind the scenes, and in so doing had extolled the virtues of the working classes over and above their so-called superiors.

'Goodness! How Quick You Were.' Wood engraving by George Du Maurier for The Hand of Ethelberta. Ethelberta *expresses surprise at how quickly Picotee fell in love with Christopher Julian. Philip V. Allingham.*

Despite the fact that Hardy had qualified as an architect and was being increasingly recognised as a man of letters, he had an inferiority complex in regard to his wife, Emma in respect of what he regarded as his humble origins. This sentiment on his part was misplaced, because his forbears were master masons who, as house builders, were just as important to society as solicitors, which was the profession of Emma's father, if not more so!

Nevertheless, Ethelberta's unwillingness to reveal to Lord Mountclere the circumstances of her 'lowly' upbringing was mirrored in Hardy's reluctance to reveal what he regarded as his humble origins to Emma.

To summarise: the real life Hardy and the fictional character Ethelberta, by marrying, represented a triumph of love over the class system.

I looked out of the window to see Rachel at work in the garden and I went out to see what she was doing.

'I've planted some fuchsias,' she said, 'to remind us of Ethelberta!' And there she was, appropriately framed by Corfe Castle in the background: Rachel, my wonderful, beautiful, and admirable real-life 'Ethelberta'!

'"In the Writing of the Composer", observed Lord Mountclere with interest.' Wood engraving by George Du Maurier for The Hand of Ethelberta. Referring to a piano composition by Christopher Julian.

28

Rachel and I Become Engaged

I TOOK Rachel to the hotel in Studland where we had first met and in the lounge, we sat down in the very same seats that we had occupied on that occasion. The waiter, a different one this time, came with the tray and once again, I asked Rachel, 'Will you be mother?' as I had done that very first time.

'I know what you're getting at,' she chuckled. 'You are hoping I will spill a drop of milk on the table, aren't you, and then summon the waiter like I did before?' I had not let her forget this incident! But this time, and somewhat to my disappointment, there were no mishaps in that respect. I now presented her with a little jewellery box and invited her to open it.

How happy she looked; happier than I have ever known her, for as we walked together along the beach, she wearing her brand-new engagement ring on the ring finger of her left hand. A giveaway was the manner in which she deported herself: her body language said it all. She walked tall, as I imagined she had done in her modelling days. If one balanced a book on that lovely head of hers, I thought, it would probably stay there. And when we got to the boat-launching ramp, she said, 'After you!' and held out her hand to help me. Whereupon, I took her arm and replied, 'No! On the contrary! After *you*!'

On the evening of the day of our engagement I took Rachel to our favourite hotel overlooking the sea, for a candlelit dinner. And afterwards over coffee, we watched the car ferry from France pass by and sail into the harbour, lit up against the night sky. In this romantic setting, she positively radiated joy. She wore a long dress with floral decoration in her favourite colour, pink. I myself had made a special effort to look smart in new shirt, new maroon-coloured cardigan which she had knitted for me, new trousers, and shoes for once, rather than trainers.

29

A Swim and a Mishap

IT HAPPENED after we had visited Studland beach for a swim and a picnic. As we were driving home in the Land Rover, Rachel let out an anguished cry. 'What is it?'

'I daren't tell you,' she said miserably. 'It's my engagement ring. I can't find it. I took it off before I went in the water, but it's not in my handbag.' She sobbed uncontrollably. I checked the vehicle to see if it had fallen on the floor, whilst she rummaged through the picnic bag. It was to no avail.

I drove to the police station in Swanage, where we were met by a young, newly-minted constable who took the details.

'Good day, Madam,' he said, and then with a smirk, 'Oh, by the way, have you had any more burglaries recently? It's all right, Madam, take no notice, I'm only joking!' The young constable was 'taking the mickey'. Rachel told me that she had once called him out to report the presence of a burglar in her house, only to discover that it was a blackbird that had flown in through an open window!

'I know it's a long shot, officer' I said, 'but my fiancée here has mislaid her engagement ring.'

'When was this, sir?'

'This morning, we believe on the beach at Studland. If anyone hands it in, could you please let us know?'

'I will, sir, certainly sir' he replied. 'We have a special box for lost property. If you would care to leave me your telephone number, I will call you if and when.'

We both needed a drink to calm our nerves, so we visited the local pub where I ordered a pint of Guinness and a large red wine for Rachel. Having returned home to Corfe, she sat beside me on the settee and I could see that she was inconsolable.

Next morning, whilst Rachel was still asleep, the telephone rang. I picked up the receiver. 'This is the Dorset Constabulary, Doctor. Someone has handed in your fiancée's ring. Could you please come and collect it at your convenience.'

After breakfast I told Rachel a white lie. 'Graham has invited me for coffee,' I said. 'Is that OK?' Whereupon I drove off in the direction of Swanage.

Having arrived at the police station I was asked to describe the ring. 'It is platinum, and in the shape of a flower, with a central diamond surrounded by a cluster of smaller diamonds,' I said. Whereupon, the policeman was satisfied, got me to sign a form, and handed it over.

It was late morning by the time I returned and Rachel was in the kitchen making lunch. Meanwhile, I made a pretence of reading a magazine. 'Food is ready,' she said. I joined her in the dining room and as she sat down, there came a shriek. 'My ring! My precious ring! It can't be!' I had placed it on a saucer next to her place setting. She jumped up, and smiling through tears of joy, said accusingly 'You knew all the time, didn't you! All the time you knew, and you kept it from me!' And the enormous hug that she gave me made it all worthwhile!

As we walked along Swanage's promenade I noticed on the shoreline a kindly father making a paper boat for his son to float on the water, just as my late father used to make for me. With the sea sparkling in the sunlight, I put my arm around Rachel's slim waist and she reached up and kissed me.

'I guess we are soulmates,' I said.

'I never want to be with anyone else, Andrew,' she said, and her loving look melted me to jelly!

As the day of our wedding approached I became more and more apprehensive. Could I really countenance it all going wrong again and face another divorce? Rachel, always intuitive, could tell that I had something on my mind, so I came right out with it. She looked mortified, and her look said it all. Words were unnecessary, but I knew what she was thinking: 'How could you possibly not trust me and my feelings for you?'

On the night before our wedding, neither of us being superstitious by nature, we slept in the same bed together. She wore a cotton nightie embroidered with little pink hearts, a present from me. On her bedside table I had placed a small posy of pussy willow and wild anemones. On my bedside table was an envelope from Rachel, silver in colour with repeating motifs of golden horseshoes. Inside was a greeting card with a little boy walking along with his arm around a little girl. I peeped inside, and the message read:

'You are my world!
You will be with me every hour of every day.
I appreciate everything you do and try to do for me.
All my love,
Your Rachel'

I treasured that card, almost more than life itself!

30

Future Plans

IN THE Market Square at Corfe Castle stands the Market Cross, which commemorates the cruel murder here of King Edward who had acceded to the throne of England at the age of twelve in the year 975. One day, we were sitting on the plinth of the Market Cross eating our ice creams when Rachel suddenly said, 'I'm worried!'

'What about?'

'Well, we're coming to the end of Ethelberta. What next?' I laughed.

'Hardy wrote 14 published novels, as you know,' I said. 'And most were set in various parts of his "Wessex", so there are 13 more to choose from! Look up there, for instance.' I pointed to the first floor bay window of a house overlooking the square.

'Ah! Lucetta's house in *The Mayor of Casterbridge*!,' said Rachel.

'A BBC TV Drama, filmed in 1978.'

'With Anna Massey as Lucetta.'

'I was thinking about Ethelberta and her marriage to Lord Mountclere,' I said. 'According to Hardy the marriage took place in Knollsea church.' 'I suppose Swanage's parish church of St Mary the Virgin was what Hardy had in mind?' Rachel looked at me quizzically. Had she guessed what was in *my* mind, I wondered?

'Oh, by the way, the Rector of Swanage says he would like to see us,' I said. Rachel looked at me in surprise.

'What for?' she said. 'After all we're not church goers.'

'Tomorrow at 11 a.m.,' I said and suddenly the penny dropped. 'You mean … ?' I nodded.

31

A Wedding!

OUR WEDDING was a quiet affair. Neither of us had relatives with whom we were in close touch, so the only people present in St Mary's church were the Rector, Graham, my best man, and Mildred, one of Rachel's former nursing colleagues. After the ceremony we went outside and posed for photographs. It was a beautiful sunny day in May when the cherry blossom was out, and it formed a backdrop to Rachel, in her matching pink dress, pink floral hat, and bouquet of pink roses!

Swanage Mill Pond and Parish Church of St Mary the Virgin by Ernest Hazlehurst, 1915.

We now set off on our honeymoon. This involved catching the little passenger ferry from Swanage Pier, traversing the wide expanse of Swanage Bay and Poole Bay, entering Poole Harbour, and journeying on up the winding River Frome to the ancient town of Wareham – Hardy's 'Anglebury'. In this, we were following in the wake of ninth-century Danish Vikings, who had sailed up the river and invaded this region in the year 875.

Our destination was the Priory Hotel, an ancient building which stood on the site of an even more venerable 'noble monasterie [monastery] of religious virgins', which was destroyed by the Danes in the year 876. The fate of the virgins may easily be surmised! The beautiful gardens of the hotel backed onto the river, where we sat and relaxed, and watched the swans drifting by, and the ducks dabbling in the reeds.

I reached into my pocket, took out a small jewellery box, and placed it on the table before her. 'For you,' I said. She lifted the lid, and inside was a necklace and pendant. 'A black pearl!' she exclaimed. 'See how it glistens!' 'It comes from Tahiti,' I said. 'And do you know what it signifies?' 'Tell me.' 'It's of a type worn by odalisques,' I continued. 'When an odalisque had completed certain ordeals, set for her by the Sultan, it was the tradition for him to reward her with a necklace of black Tahitian pearls to signify her new found dignity and status. However. I'm afraid that I could only afford one pearl. Sorry!'

'Allow me,' I said, and I hung the necklace around her neck. I had no need of thanks. I saw the loving look in her eyes and that was thanks enough. 'But I don't deserve it,' she said, gazing at me earnestly. 'After all, I haven't gone through any ordeals.' 'Oh yes you have,' I replied. 'The ordeal of having to put up with me all this time!'

Here in Wareham, known as 'The Gateway to Purbeck', were several connections to Thomas Hardy. For example, the Anglebury House tea rooms where T. E. Lawrence once regularly occupied his favourite seat by the window (which is now commemorated with a plaque). Hardy and Lawrence were bosom friends, and the hero of the Desert War often called at Max Gate to visit the great man of letters, roaring up the driveway on his legendary 'Brough Superior' motorcycle.

And it was to Wareham – 'Anglebury' – that Ethelberta came, 'across meadows fed by the Froom' – River Frome – and travelled onwards, crossing the railway line and entering 'a lonely heath'.

32

The Changing Face of Swanage

DID HARDY ever return to Swanage – his 'Knollsea' – I wondered, after what for him was clearly an interesting and productive time as he completed *The Hand of Ethelberta*? Yes, because in September 1892, Hardy and Emma arrived at Swanage train station with members of the Dorset Field Club. Whereupon, George Burt conducted the party to Durlston Castle for luncheon.

In 1919, the year after the First World War ended, Hardy attended the opening of 'Steepways' Red Cross Children's Hospital, Peveril Road, not far from West End Cottage, by Dr Frederick Ridgway the Bishop of Salisbury. This was for the children of Dorset men who had served or were currently serving their country as members of the armed forces. What changes would Hardy have noticed, between 1875 and 1919?

In 1881, George Burt had a new Town Hall built in the High Street on the site of the old one. 'But not content with that,' I told Rachel, 'for its façade he used the façade of the Mercers Hall in Cheapside, a street in the City of London, which the Mowlem Company had been contracted to demolish in a road widening project.'

'Little London by the sea again!' she said.

'And guess who the architect was? G. R. Crickmay, Hardy's former employer.'

'So Hardy would have felt quite at home here!' said Rachel, laughing.

In that same year, a new lighthouse was constructed at Anvil Point.

Hardy and Emma had arrived in Swanage in 1892, having travelled by train. The Southampton to Dorchester line had opened in 1847. Nearly four decades later, on 20 May 1885, the first train ran from Swanage to Wareham, via Corfe Castle, and a public holiday was declared!

Burt's Durlston Castle, to which Hardy was invited in September 1892, was built in 1887/8, and the 'Great Globe in 1887. 'Let's go and take a closer look,' said Rachel.

Constructed of the finest Portland stone, the Great Globe weighs 40 tons, is 10 feet in diameter and set on a plinth. It was constructed in 15 segments in John Mowlem's stone yard in Greenwich, the segments being fixed together by granite dowels. It was then brought to Swanage by sea and assembled. Set into the wall behind the Great Globe are stone tablets engraved with verses from the poets, and other snippets of information, such as: 'The swallow flies at the rate of 100 mph. The carrier pigeon flies at the rate of 40 mph.'

Set into the south-facing wall of the castle itself are more stone plaques engraved with more information. As we examined them closely, I said, 'Why did George Burt find it necessary to inform visitors to Durlston Castle of the maximum rise and fall of tides, for example, at Wexford, Ireland?'

'And what the time was in various cities of the world, for example Calcutta, when it was noon at Greenwich?' said Rachel.

The tablets were also engraved with a great deal of astronomical information. This was probably obtained from Burt's uncle, John Mowlem whose hobby was astronomy and who, atop his retirement home in Swanage High Street, had erected an astronomical observatory.

Subsequent to the building of Durlston Castle and the Great Globe, Burt purchased the land to the west as far as Anvil Point, on which he hoped to build a luxury housing estate. This did not come to pass. However, at intervals along the cliff path between the two, are more stone tablets with more 'improving texts'. It's as if George Burt, having risen from humble beginnings, was anxious to display his knowledge and be thought of as a man of the world; hence Hardy's appellation, 'King of Swanage!'

Rachel and I walked along the cliff path until we came to Tilly Whim, with the lighthouse at Anvil Point visible just across a valley to the west. This former cliff quarry operated from about the year 1700 until 1812. The name 'Whim' derives from the eponymous name of the wooden derrick, which was used to lower the stone into waiting boats below.

In 1887 the enterprising and imaginative George Burt created a new entrance to the cliff quarry, using explosives to blast through the rock. It was now possible for visitors to his Durlston Estate to descend from the cliff path down a flight of stone steps to the ledges overhanging the sea.

The lighthouse, Anvil Point by Ernest Hazlehurst, 1915.

However, the entrance to the quarry is now barred by an iron gate, it being no longer safe to descend into it from the cliff path owing to the danger of rock falls.

'Guess who was here before us?' said Rachel.

'Not the ubiquitous Thomas Hardy?' I said. 'But how do you know?'

'I came across a reference to an unfinished watercolour painting by him of Tilly Whim,' said Rachel. 'Here's a copy of it.'

'It looks to me as if Hardy was halfway down the cliff on the ledge when he did the painting,' I said.

George Burt died in 1894 at the age of seventy-eight. In 1897 a new pier was constructed, primarily for the use of paddle steamers.

The First World War ended on 11 November 1918, the year preceding Hardy's visit to Swanage in 1919. His wife, Emma had died seven years earlier on 27 November 1912 aged seventy-two. During the war troop trains brought soldiers to Swanage station where they entered various training camps in the vicinity. The Swanage war memorial contains the names of 99 Swanage men who lost their lives in that conflict.

Our honeymoon was coming to an end. 'Shall we ever get Thomas Hardy out of our system,' asked Rachel with a smile, as we sipped our wine and watched the local youths jumping off Wareham's Frome Bridge and dive-bombing the ducks. 'Why would we ever wish to?' I retorted.

'Quite!,' she said. 'Why would we ever wish to?'